Credit Insurance

Credit Insurance

Miran Jus

AMSTERDAM • BOSTON • HEIDELBERG • LONDON
NEW YORK • OXFORD • PARIS • SAN DIEGO
SAN FRANCISCO • SINGAPORE • SYDNEY • TOKYO
Academic Press is an imprint of Elsevier

Academic Press is an imprint of Elsevier
The Boulevard, Langford Lane, Kidlington, Oxford, OX5 1GB, UK
225 Wyman Street, Waltham, MA 02451, USA

First published 2013

The views, interpretations and opinions expressed in this book are entirely those
of the author. Whilst to the best of the author's knowledge, every reasonable effort has
been made to avoid errors and omissions as well as to ensure accuracy, information
contained in the book may not be comprehensive. Therefore, readers should not use it
or act upon it without appropriate professional advice and additional instructions
from their experienced credit insurance brokers or advisers.

Notices
Knowledge and best practice in this field are constantly changing. As new research and
experience broaden our understanding, changes in research methods, professional practices,
or medical treatment may become necessary.

Practitioners and researchers must always rely on their own experience and knowledge in
evaluating and using any information, methods, compounds, or experiments described herein.
In using such information or methods they should be mindful of their own safety and the safety
of others, including parties for whom they have a professional responsibility.

To the fullest extent of the law, neither the Publisher nor the authors, contributors, or editors,
assume any liability for any injury and/or damage to persons or property as a matter of products
liability, negligence or otherwise, or from any use or operation of any methods, products,
instructions, or ideas contained in the material herein.

British Library Cataloguing-in-Publication Data
A catalogue record for this book is available from the British Library

Library of Congress Cataloging-in-Publication Data
A catalog record for this book is available from the Library of Congress

ISBN: 978-0-12-411458-6

For information on all Academic Press publications
visit our website at **store.elsevier.com**

This book has been manufactured using Print On Demand technology. Each copy is produced
to order and is limited to black ink. The online version of this book will show color figures
where appropriate.

Working together to grow
libraries in developing countries

www.elsevier.com | www.bookaid.org | www.sabre.org

ELSEVIER   BOOK AID
            International   Sabre Foundation

Transferred to Digital Printing in 2013

CONTENTS

LIST OF ABBREVIATIONS

ABCP	asset-backed commercial papers
ALASECE	Asociación Latinoamericana de Segura de Credito
ART	alternative risk transfer
BC	before Christ
B/E	bill of exchange
B/L	bill of lading
B2B	business-to-business
CAD (C/D)	cash against documents
CDS	credit default swaps
CEN	confiscation, expropriation, and nationalization
CIF	cost, insurance, and freight
CWO	cash with order
CWP	claims waiting period
D/A	documents against acceptance
D/ICPO	documents against irrevocable confirmed payment order
D/P	documents against payment
ECA	export credit agency
EUR	Euro
FDI	foreign direct investment
FOB	free on board
GDP	gross domestic product
HOR	horizon of risk
ICIEC	Islamic Corporation for the Insurance of Investment and Export Credit
ICISA	International Credit Insurance and Surety Association
IML	insurer's maximum liability
IS	information system
IT	information technology
((C)(I)(R)) L/C	((confirmed) (ir)(revocable)) letter of credit
MIGA	Multilateral Investment Guarantee Agency
NPV	net present value
OECD	Organization for Economic Cooperation and Development

OJ	official journal
PC	percentage of cover
PCR	precredit risk
PRI	political risk insurance
Q.B.(D.)	Queen's Bench (Division)
ROT	retention of title
SDR	special drawing rights
SME	small- and medium-sized enterprise
UK	United Kingdom
VAT	value added tax
WTO	World Trade Organization
XL	excess (of) loss ((re)insurance)

LIST OF FIGURES

In 1984, Miran Jus graduated from the faculty of law at the University of Ljubljana, Slovenia; in 1989, he received an M.A. in economics from the faculty of economics at the University of Zagreb; and in 2002, he obtained his Ph.D. (LL.D.) from the Faculty of Law at the University of Ljubljana. In his career, he has served as a diplomat, executive director for research and strategy of Slovenian Export Credit Agency and independent legal and financial consultant, acquiring wealth of experience in international trade, business law, and finance. Currently, he is an executive director for structured financing and legal affairs in a power engineering company, Korona, Inc. He has published several books and over 180 articles and other works on the law of international payments, export credit and investment insurance, monetary, banking and insurance law, trade and project finance, risk management, etc. He is also a member of Council of Experts of Slovenian Insurance Supervision Agency, an assistant professor of business law at the Faculty of Economics at the University of Ljubljana, an arbitrator and a speaker at conferences, seminars and workshops dealing with various legal, economic, and financial issues.

CHAPTER 1

Introduction

Companies use **credit insurance** as one of the **personal securities** and frequently used high-quality means of protection against **payment risks**, that is, the possibility that the buyer (debtor) will not make payment for goods and services in full and in a timely fashion. These risks are economic phenomena of nonnegligible proportions thus influencing the business success. Effective protection against the debtors' insolvency and default risks is one of the key factors for success in business operations.

The principal motive of companies is to make profit. The latter in general depends on the revenues and expenses resulting from the business operations. However, sound business decisions must give consideration to other factors as well, for example, indirect benefits and the **risks of business transactions**. Unless a company is adequately insured against the risks, the consequence may be losses which increase expenses, threaten profitability of business transactions, and the success of the company. Losses increase costs, reduce the profit or even eat away the capital of the company, and threatens its liquidity, solvency, or mere existence.

Credit insurers can provide companies with the required security for their business operations where risks—which will to a certain extent always exist (*No risk—no fun!*)—would be brought into line with revenues, other incomes, and assets of the company.

Terminology: Risk

Risk (*risico/risqué/risiko/periculum...*) is a word of an Italian origin and a constituent part of the insurance contract. For the insured or his insurable interest to be protected against the risk, it is also the *"causa"* of the contract, while the existence of the risks is the foundation and precondition of the contractual relations between the insurer and the insured.

As this phenomenon is highly complex and exists in several forms, that is, pure risk, where uncertain future event results in loss or speculative risk and where the circumstances may lead to loss or profit, it is difficult to provide uniform explanation. Therefore, we will try to indicate the definition which may be well used in credit insurance: the risk is future's uncertain and

Credit Insurance. DOI: http://dx.doi.org/10.1016/B978-0-12-411458-6.00001-0

unforeseen natural phenomena or event—act or omission (*commissio/ ommissio*) or circumstances—bound to state, companies, individuals, or things, whose consequence for the company is material and/or nonmaterial loss if the company is not adequately insured against it.

●●●

The rule of the contemporary business transactions: *Buy now, pay later.*

Trade without **credit** is almost inconceivable. Credit which is a word with many meanings (depending on the context in which it appears), loan and sale credit, is the *lifeblood* of a highly competitive contemporary business environment and a necessity for business operations as well as undisturbed trade flows. Today, we can talk about monetary economy and to a large extent also about credit-based economy where selling on credit terms is a requirement—*Customer is the king!*—imposed to the companies and brought on by harsh international competition. As the volume of trade is increasing, issues of trade finance, buyers' and suppliers' credits, and inherent risks as well as accessory credit insurance are becoming the concern of many business operators.

●●●

Enterprises live (and sometimes die) by credit. (Prof. Goode, Commercial Law (1995), p. 635)

Payment—insolvency and default—risks are inherent to each credit transaction or sales on deferred payment terms. Credit risk and insurance against these risks thus become an even more important factor to be considered for the contemporary business operations. In commercial transactions on credit terms or trade financing, creditors with inadequate insurance cover remain exposed to a wide array of risks spectrum. There is always a possibility that delivered goods or services performed would not be paid for by the customer or principal and/or interests would not be repaid by the debtor, that is, the debtor simply does not pay his/her due debts (*mora solvendi*) under the terms and conditions or in the place as agreed upon in the underlying commercial or financial contract (*peius*). Such nonpayment, delayed payment, insolvency, or debtor's default are quite common in practice and could turn the creditor into financial disaster and ruin. Even though careful selection of business partners and thoroughly stipulated commercial contracts may diminish the risks, the vendor selling its goods or services in terms of deferred payment is usually not fully protected against the above risks without collateral or additional first-class securities. When the delivered goods are no longer in the supplier's possession, the buyer's contractual obligations *per se* do not guarantee that the seller will be actually paid.

●●●
───

Ancy's rule (Who is Ancy?): *There is no trade without credit—and no credit without risk!*
───

Credit (*del credere*) insurance has developed into an appreciated risk mitigation tool for industrialists or merchants, and is meant for protecting trade receivables—an important part of a company's assets—against the broad spectrum of commercial and noncommercial risks. With credit insurance, sellers are able to trade soundly, despite unfavorable economic or political situations, customer bankruptcy, or poor payment discipline. In the past, credit insurance had been considered an esoteric insurance type well understood only by few in the business community with a reputation of being complicated. However, with rapidly evolving credit insurance market and competition among credit insurers, development of services, and information technology (IT), they have made the supply of these services more flexible, cut down prices, improved the response time of the insurers, and through simplifications made credit insurance less complex, user-friendly, and more customized and accessible for the companies. Modern credit insurance makes business, credit risk management, and debt collection easier, thus stimulating the companies on a global level to use it more and more frequently. Higher risk and product awareness has led to increased demand for credit insurance as a risk mitigation tool and it has gained global recognition.

●●●
───

If we are adequately insured against risk, there is no hazard!
───

CHAPTER 2

What Is Credit Insurance and What Does It Offer?

Insurance helps creditors to have a good night's sleep!

2.1 DEFINITION

For suppliers selling goods and services in domestic or foreign markets on credit or deferred payment terms, credit insurance provides insurance coverage for outstanding trade receivables against the nonpayment risk of their customers or debtors and their eventual guarantors.

By concluding a credit insurance contract, exporters or sellers—that is, creditors of underlying sales and other commercial contracts—may partly or completely transfer commercial and/or noncommercial risks of business transactions to the specialized financial institution (credit insurance company). Such credit and/or manufacturing risks may cause damage (*damnum*), which could be in exchange for insurance premium compensated by insurer's claims paid. Indemnification for loss sustained shall be made within the predetermined amount, if the seller (insured creditor/obligee) without his own fault is not paid by his domestic or foreign buyers (debtors/obligors or guarantors) for his goods or services

Credit Insurance. DOI: http://dx.doi.org/10.1016/B978-0-12-411458-6.00002-2

sold on credit terms. As a condition for claim payment, such material loss incurred has to be caused by the insured event, for example, if the risk of nonpayment materializes due to permanent insolvency or protracted default of the debtor, which according to general and special insurance conditions represent specified insured event (including repudiation or buyer's refusal to accept goods, political events, and other noncommercial risks). Figure 2.1 illustrates the credit insurance of underlying trade receivables, its participants, and their relations.

Should we attempt to classify insurance according to the insured subject matter (property insurance, personal insurance, and liability insurance), then credit insurance as one of the insurance classes belongs to the **property insurance** as accounts receivable from trade credits represent company's assets—to be more precise in the **credit insurance and suretyship subgroup** (in a wider sense of the word fidelity insurance is also a part of this insurance class).

However, credit insurance may be perceived as quite different from other types of insurance, not just in the underwriting sense due to special nature of credit risks involved but in the legal sense as well. The fact that credit insurance involves more or less equal contractual parties and specific particularities of the credit insurance are the main reasons why

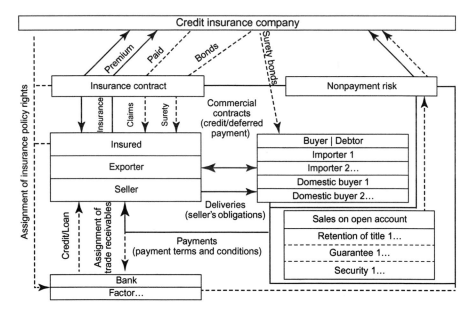

Figure 2.1 Credit insurance and its participants.

certain provisions of governing Civil Codes on insurance contracts do not apply always for credit insurance (except sometimes by analogy), while contractual obligations of the parties are defined in detail within the insurance contracts and general credit insurance conditions. **Legal sources** for credit insurance must therefore not only be looked for in applicable substantive laws but also mainly in applicable general and special insurance conditions, business customs, and informal legal sources ("soft laws"), as well as in case law.

Brief History of Credit Insurance

Credit insurance has a relatively long history or *prehistory*. Its origins can already be found in early economies, when people started to cooperate in order to prevent danger and/or render the damage in distance trade, as was the case of Chinese merchants when vessels sank in the rapids of the Yangtze around 3000 BC. The next example is the Hamurabi's Code of Law (approximately 1700 BC), which provided that the caravan leaders were jointly and severally liable for the eventual damage caused by robberies. The roots of credit insurance can also be found at the Greek island Rhodes, ancient India, from the heritage of maritime law, institute of general average (coming from Roman law and surviving up to the present date), medieval guilds, *maritime loans* known from the Roman law (*foenus*), from which the marine insurance policies evolved (the first known marine insurance policy was written in Genoa and is dated from 1347) and the first marine insurance companies in Paris (1668) and London, for example, Lloyd's from the seventeenth century. The founder of the credit insurance theory is **Paris Sanguinetti** (1839—*Essai d'une nouvelle théorie pour appliquer le système des assurances aux dommages sur les faillites*).

Aiming to please their clients, marine insurers issued insurance policies which guaranteed payment when goods reached their destination. **The first credit insurance policy**, or at least the oldest preserved one, is supposed to be issued by the **Banco Adriatico di Sicurta from Trieste on the 6th of December 1831**, while other sources claim that the first credit insurance policy was issued by the British Commercial Insurance Company, founded in 1820 otherwise offering mostly fire and life insurances. The Banque Mallet et. C. from Paris in 1848 founded L'Union du Commerce. This was doomed to be a failure like some of the succeeding credit insurance companies, as they were operating according to bank principles, that is, without the selection of bad risks. The first whole turnover credit insurance policy was supposedly issued in England in 1885. Credit insurance with the states' support included developed after the First World War, when exporters were insecure to trade with formerly hostile countries and found its place in Europe around 1890 (in those times Lloyd's started to insure credit risk) because Australia encountered serious financial problems. However, it must be mentioned that two specialized credit insurance companies (Commercial Credit Mutual Assurance Association and Solvency Mutual Guarantee) had already been founded in 1852. They were followed by credit insurers in other countries, for example, ECGD in the UK was established in 1919 and German Hermes (today as Euler Hermes, being the largest credit insurer in the world) was founded in 1917. The latter was one of the first insurance companies to conclude in 1926 an agreement enabling it to provide export credit insurance on the state account.

INTERNATIONAL ORGANIZATIONS. As a result of the first international conference on credit insurance, which took place in London in 1926, the first international organization of private credit insurers and reinsurers was established in 1928. In the 1950s, this nongovernmental organization was joined by the surety companies to form the present International Credit Insurance and Surety Association (**ICISA**); some of its member are also the members of 1972 established Pan-American Surety Association (**PASA**) and the 1982 created regional organization Asociación Latinoamericana de Segura de Credito (**ALASECE**). In 1934, the International Union of Credit and Investment Insurers (**Berne Union**)—global nongovernmental international organization of the Export Credit Agencies (ECAs) with the seat in London was founded, consisting of 49 members in 2010 who were until recently in some or other way linked with the governments for at least part of their business and complement credit insurance from private sector. Berne Union fosters sound principles of export credit and investment insurance and encourages common understanding and exchange of information and expertise among members. Nowadays, the organization's members are also some major private credit and investment (re)insurers and the World Bank affiliate Multilateral Investment Guarantee Agency (MIGA); a similar international organization − not global but regional − is the Islamic Corporation for the Insurance of Investments and Export Credit (ICIEC), a subsidiary of Islamic Development Bank established in 1994 with 40 shareholders from Arab, African, Asian, and other countries. Berne Union is also the godfather of the **Prague Club**, which harbors some of the younger ECAs, members of Berne Union, and newly established ECAs from Central, Eastern, and Southeastern Europe as well as other members from Asia and Africa (in 2010, 33 in total).

Obviously credit insurance has developed from, and together with, transport insurance and increased importance in the period of industrial revolution when entrepreneurship and trade boomed. The number of companies increased and business was less and less concluded on the basis of long-standing relationships, while the competition forced the companies to sell their goods on credit terms. Today credit insurance is widespread all over the world and above all in Europe. The size of this extremely concentrated market is estimated on more than USD 5 billion and according to predictions its growth rate is estimated at 2.5 times the average growth rate of the world economy.

REINSURANCE. The development of **reinsurance industry**, known in the world from the fourteenth century, was also important for the development of credit insurance. Due to reinsurers' financial strength and risk dispersion, it was possible to cover extremely large losses and numerous loss-causing events. Reinsurance is therefore the backbone of developed credit insurance industry; without it and without reduced underwriting risks for primary insurance, credit insurance could not be conducted on its present scale. Regardless of the cyclical nature of private reinsurance market and reinsurers' appetite for this "peripheral business," some larger reinsurers are entering more and more actively in credit insurance market. They increasingly underwrite commercial risks and to some extent also political and other noncommercial risks on a substantial and growing scale, but majority of them are rarely willing to reinsure political risks only and require these risks to be offered to them together with the ceded commercial risks. Due to the idiosyncratic nature of noncommercial risks and because political risk insurance is a highly specialized type of insurance, it requires *inter alia* special underwriting criteria and insurance capacities and is provided to exporters and investors mainly by specialized private credit insurance companies and ECAs enjoining full faith and credit of the governments.

2.2 FUNCTIONS OF CREDIT INSURANCE

Insurance plays an important role and has vital importance on the safety of life as well as for the security and success of business operations. It spreads losses over large numbers of those exposed to risks and such diversification and distribution of risks also takes place geographically and over time. Insurance comes to our mind especially when we feel threatened and even more so should the risk be existential, and the value of the goods at risk (economic security gained by the insurance) is rising in our estimation. On the other hand, the **insurance** belongs to **superior goods**, with their growth of demand correlated with the growth of disposable income. From an expert point of view, the insurance may seem complex, complicated, and also boring; however, this does not hold true for credit insurance, as it is nowadays more widely understood and inseparably linked with many diverse business relations and events.

Insurance, and likewise reinsurance, do not primarily reduce the risk or prevent loss-causing events, except indirectly due to their preventive and curative functions and effects.

By legal means and actions, one can only eliminate or transfer some risks as legal facts, but the probability of a loss-causing event may be diminished or reduced by the rule with real actions only. Just like most other financial instruments, credit insurance does not eliminate risks but mainly transfers them to stronger partners: financial institutions. The national economy may also benefit from credit insurance as specialized financial institutions with their skills, capacities, and financial strength are capable enough of bearing and managing the risks underwritten.

Insurance undeniably reduces the material consequences of loss-causing events with its most important **active function**, which is the insurer's "financial guarantee" for indemnification and claims paid, that certainly give the companies (insured parties) their required economic security in risk-involved business operations. However, and in addition, insurance **preventive** and **curative functions** may also reduce the likelihood of losses or facilitate the mitigation of their consequences for policyholders. On the other hand, companies do not only rely upon credit insurance to avoid and mitigate risk, but also to enable them to cooperate with providers of financial and other services, that is, commercial banks, factors and other financial institutions, credit rating agencies, consultants, lawyers, and debt collection agencies.

Export and domestic credit insurance are oiling the wheels of trade and provide complete and integral financial services with different functions and several activities. Credit insurance does not only support companies in their business operations and serves as an instrument of risk management covering the damage caused by nonpayment of their buyers ("reparation") and thus protects their finances and balance sheets, but also offers policyholders the benefits of many other extra services that become a necessity for successful business.

AUXILIARY SERVICES. These related and additional insurance services are even more important for credit insurance than for other insurance classes. With the aid of additional services offered by credit insurers, entrepreneurs can outsource some activities and can better focus on their basic activities, such as expansion in new markets, acquisition of new customers, and development of products and services. Likewise, for example, with the accessible credit information databases, credit insurers dispose a wealth of experience and expertise in technical aspects of trade and trade finance, and can therefore be cost-effective focal points for the companies to share such expertise with the insurers. These unbundled auxiliary services of traditional competing products, such as credit information, risk monitoring, invoicing, and debt collection, are sometimes provided by credit insurers separately or may be included in the package of credit insurance services—the so-called **serviced credit insurance**, that is, credit insurance products and services in many varieties beyond the traditional notion of insurance.

Credit insurers are **protectors of the insured companies against credit risks** and at the same time they are **trustworthy long-term partners** providing safe business, operating efficiency, and opportunities for growth and development. Credit insurers protect the policyholder's cash flow, income and profit, balance sheets and market position thus providing opportunities for expansion on new and existing markets as well as acquisition of new customers.
The confidence in business is usually hard to obtain and easy to lose!

Nonpayment of bad debts and late payments grow trade risk. These not only affect the finances of the companies (accounts receivable of typical nonfinancial company are estimated at 30 percent of its assets but may with ease reach up to 35 or 40 percent or even more), but also leads to additional costs and loss of time spent in debt collection, which may in the end even surpass direct financial losses caused by nonpayment of the buyer. Buyer's payment default has additional adverse side effects linked to borrowings and costs of bridge financing, due to provoked cash-flow problems.

2.2.1 General—Sales and Exports Promotion

●●●
_____

Credits boost sales while credit insurance provides companies with security.

_____

Propulsive companies are usually strongly involved in trade and, due to specialization, the benefits of exchange are fruitful for participants in business transactions as well as for national economy. Growth potential and competitive market pressures are key forces pushing enterprises into this worldwide arena with its inherent risks.

LEGAL ENVIRONMENT. To perform safe and successful business activities, companies require confidence and legal security as well as properly stipulated commercial contracts with clearly, precisely, and unambiguously defined contractual obligations of both parties. Equally important is that obligations are fulfilled (*pacta sunt servanda*) or adequately penalized by law or contract in case of nonperformance or breach of contract. The legal system alone usually gives contract parties certain legal protection (*remedium*) against these business risks, for example:

i. Right to demand the fulfilment of obligations (unless the so-called common law privilege exists).
ii. The party which remains true to the contract is given the opportunity to withdraw from the contract (*ultima ratio*), and in addition to the seller's right of avoidance also file the reparation claim if the contract was partly fulfilled.
iii. Demand to remedy the defects or to reduce the contract price.
iv. Claim to compensate for damages.
v. Default interest.
vi. Objections against the nonperformance of counterparty (*exceptio non adimpledi contractus*).
vii. Objection of endangerment and right to suspend performance, etc.

Furthermore, contracting parties have the opportunity to include certain legal institutes in their commercial contracts to enhance, harden, and secure contractual obligations, for example, agreed downpayment, cash deposit, penalties, and liquidated damages. Unfortunately, the faith in almightiness of the legal norms and contractual provisions in practice is often just an illusion (incompleteness of contracts). Certain conditions imposed by applicable laws and/or contract clauses must be fulfilled in order to use these institutes and make them binding, effective, and enforceable. However, business operators often find it impossible or hard to fulfill, for instance to prove the damage or extent of loss sustained and counterparty's liability. On the other hand, sometimes contractual obligations and legal sanctions may not be carried out because of the debtor's insolvency or expiration of period of limitation. Moreover, judicial and execution proceedings are usually demanding and expensive, while the outcome is often uncertain, especially in foreign and difficult markets and jurisdictions.

Therefore, it is a common business practice to give special attention to various risk protective instruments, all the more in business operations with time gap between the stipulation and solution phases and operations where debtor's liability becomes due after the supplier of goods or services has already fulfilled his obligations, for example, in trade on credit or deferred payment terms.

TRADE DILEMMA. Companies need first to spend money on production factors and have to bridge the gap between the outlay of funds and revenues from sales with internal and/or external finances. Trade relations were thus always dealing with fundamental **trade dilemma:** who (seller, buyer, or both) should finance trade with his own and/or external financial means. Distance trade makes simultaneousness of prestations for contracting parties almost impossible. As a rule, one contracting party credits the counterparty, while the decision to grant the credit is tightly connected with business transaction risk sharing between seller and buyer. The first one has, "*ceteris paribus,*", interest to obtain downpayment agreed upon or to receive full payment before or on delivery, while the buyer's opposite interest is to takeover the goods of a proper quality and quantity and let the seller finance the transaction. In other words, buyers usually do not want to pay until they receive the goods (or at least before receiving the title to them) and want to pay for the goods as late as possible after the inspection of goods or even after delivered goods are already sold to final buyer. Each party wants assurance that the other party will fulfill its obligations properly. The final decision is taken in negotiations and according to a mutual agreement of contracting parties. The decisive factors of negotiations are market position, business, and other relations between seller and buyer, usages, and negotiating position, as well as some financial factors, for example, availability of internal financial means, access to bank loans, and interest rates available.

BUYERS' MARKETS. When we talk about the world economy, we frequently talk about the **buyers' markets** with market situation and negotiating positions being mostly in favor of buyers, who strive to improve their cash flow with deferred payment purchasing. In order to expand or sometimes even to maintain existing markets, sellers are forced to grant credits, as capital is scarce and many buyers are only willing to conclude the deal when trade financing is offered. Trade is therefore oftentimes financed by the exporter alone, or with the help of banking facilities, factoring or other external financing. Today trade credits are usually the easiest accessible source of external financing for the companies and buying on credit from suppliers is the single largest source of short-term company debt.

Modern economies are monetary and to large extent **credit-based systems**, using credits to bridge the time gap and physical distances between production, distribution, and consumption of goods. Contemporary business practice treats trade receivables as an important transition phase between deliveries and payments.

●●●

Credit creates additional purchasing power.

COMPETITIVE ADVANTAGES. The ability to offer the sales on credit terms is frequently the most important factor in winning new business. Favorable credit terms, as a part of seller's supply package, give the company competitive advantage toward other suppliers of goods and services. Thanks to credit insurance cover, the insured may be in a position to offer supplier credit, while their competitors might not have such possibility. The sellers who insist, for example, on cash or letters of credit payment for their shipments are likely to lose orders to other more competitive suppliers. Buyers are less and less willing to commit their working capital to back their banks' letters of credit which are, on the other hand, also costly and burden their credit limits. **Credits extended to buyers, favorable credit terms, and deferred payment sales, possibly on open account basis and without additional securities— that is, clean payment, together with the marketable potential of goods and frequent buyer's lack of working capital for cash payments in the harsh competitive environment, are often at least as important as other elements of competition (*conditio sine qua non*), that is, product price and quality, delivery terms, and manufacturer's or supplier's warranties**. Many business deals are never made just because of offered unfavorable payment terms and conditions accompanied with collateral and other requested securities. Due to uncertainty, the seller's risk in trade on deferred payment terms is often simply too big.

Even though business cooperation between companies usually runs smoothly or at least without any big problems, a certain level of risk always exists and the occurrence of loss-causing event can be an unpleasant surprise. Even though a bed is considered a safe place, as a matter of fact, most people die in it.

It is considered a golden rule that there is no commercial business without credit, but unfortunately no credit without risk. Companies can often hardly bear the risks of business transactions on their own without endangering their security and profitability. Suppliers' credits and sales on credit or deferred payment terms immobilize more or less limited financial means, but at the same time companies cannot allow themselves to have big assets tied in debts. Companies' reserves and capital are not unlimited. Therefore, they cannot afford to write-off debts too frequently or in large amounts because the required average profit rate in harsh competition does not allow such yielding and sometimes it is also not economically justified to let the accounts receivable exceed certain level as they cut down the yield coefficient and the company's assets. The risk transfer to the third persons, that is, the credit insurers, therefore creates potential for growth and offers a company a chance to increase its capacities and efficiency. By added value of credit insurance services, credit insurance gives the clients a chance to grasp market opportunities by **increasing the sales numbers** with existing and new customers.

RISK ATTITUDE. Companies do not share the same approach and do not apply the same level of protection against the different risks. They can be risk averse or risk lovers, for example, from one extreme—*full protection* by all means to another extreme, that is, no protection against certain risks at all when the companies decide not to insure themselves. Some of them are thrifty and save on insurance premiums, speculating the loss-causing event would not occur or the damage would be minor and manageable for their capacities and capabilities. Nevertheless, the decision on insurance, its extent, and insurance conditions, as well as use of other protective devices, should not be automatically neglected and must always be based on rational grounds.

●●●

Sale is not accomplished until the obligations of parties are fulfilled—delivered goods are paid for.

Lenders are expecting that their loans will be repaid by the borrowers on the due dates. Sellers, who trade on deferred payment terms, assume that their trade receivables (*nomen*) would be paid at maturity. In other words, sellers (creditors) expect the fulfillment (*solutio*) of the debt payment for delivered goods or services rendered. Based on this expectation, they can hire loans, but in the case of nonpayments or payment delays, they may fall in serious trouble. Sales statistics alone do not tell us much if the company does not get such debts paid. To sell *per se* may not and should not be the final goal of companies and as a matter of fact, it is usually not the hardest part of the task—except in waste exports which must be paid by the supplier. In business practice companies often overlook that the sold goods and services must be paid for and the salesmen received their bonuses for deals they made. Sales as such are the most important for poorly managed companies that put aside payments and risks. **In fact the goods are sold only when they are fully paid for**.

●●●────────────────────────────────────

Credit is not a grant and it should not be given as a gift!

The above statement was confirmed by anecdotal evidence of many vendors who were left "empty handed," despite having "excellent" customers and first-class relations with "good and strong" business partners, based on the many years of personal acquaintance and operating on *safe markets* in developed countries. Many of them considered that no credit insurance is needed for their business, but the attitude of some of them proved to be wrong. Let us just remember the scandals and bankruptcies of renowned companies such as Enron, General Motors, WorldCom, Moulinex, Grunding, Quelle, and Parmalat. Reputable and profitable companies may also become bankrupt if their problems with cash-flow escalate. Some of the companies—bad payers—come from the branches heavily affected by recession, depending on elasticity of demand for their products and some otherwise healthy companies may have problems with payment discipline of their customers and consequently they cannot pay their own debts (*knock-on insolvencies* or *domino effect*). It is also well known that the liquidity problems are passed down the supply chain from financially constrained customers to their suppliers and *vice versa*.

Numerous companies have very concentrated trade patterns and depend heavily on one or two key customers; their situation may become even worse if they are dependent on suppliers who have found themselves in serious trouble, liquidity shocks, or bankruptcy procedures. Speaking from experience, newly-founded SMEs commonly have less access to bank finance and have more problems because many go bankrupt in the first years. However, there are also *per se* trustworthy customers operating from high-risk countries, which *volens nolens* influence their business, reputation, and credit rating.

Trade credit normally means that the seller takes the risk of nonpayment until the owed debt is settled. His buyer will not pay outstanding debt and so the goods sold on credit would be given as a *gift*. Of course, such nasty shocks and perils are not welcome and this is not the sellers' goal, for they are not charities but companies who strive to make profit. Payment defaults do not only influence the financial statements of the companies but may also lead to additional costs connected with debt collection and recoveries. The costs of invoicing and bad debt collection may reduce the profit of the company by 2−3 percent and there are also the costs of bridge finance borrowings to be considered. **Direct and indirect costs of poor credit risk management may be extremely high.**

Nonpayment of delivered goods means that the company must cover the loss of income with other businesses, which is by no means easy, and find new customers or distributors at the same time. Therefore, the company with bad buyers (debtors) might not get any return on previous marketing activities.

Examples:

- To cover the relatively small overdue debt of EUR 20,000.00, a company with a 4 percent profit before taxation must increase its turnover by approximately EUR 500,000.00 (quite a considerable amount).
- Annual loss of the company caused by the buyer's default amounts to EUR 22,500.00. At the annual turnover of EUR 1.5 million and at an anticipated 5 percent profit rate, a company aiming to compensate the lost profit would have to increase its annual turnover as much as 30 percent.

●●●

The word "credit (*credere/creditum*)" is of Latin origin and means faith, trust.
Faith may be naivety and trust can be betrayed.

●●●

Trust is good, but the adequate insurance is even better!

Credit insurance can provide risk enhancement. Therefore, it becomes more and more an essential prerequisite for acquiring of businesses and their successful completion. Credit insurance guarantees economic security and can increase sales through securing the anticipated cash flow and consequently positively affects the development of the company and its business success. On a macroeconomic level, credit insurance can increase trade and exchange with positive impact on GDP, while in international trade significant positive effects and impressive multipliers of credit insurance on total exports is also proven.

The seller capable of offering goods or services on demanding foreign or domestic markets on deferred payment terms on open account basis— and without additional securities as the result of credit insurance—**will have significant advantage over competitors** who avoid such payment terms and conditions or require some other bank instruments. Trading on open account and not insisting on collateral may show the creditor's trust in buyer who does not need to know that the supplier's credits are insured.

Credit insurance can improve the buyers' access to supplier credits, that is, one of the most favorable sources of external financing, and hence credit insurers can also be seen as "invisible banks." Credit insured sellers may sometimes also agree to more flexible conditions in their underlying commercial contracts, for example, to allow shipment as soon as the goods are ready and changes of shipping and trade documents can be agreed between the contract parties solely without involving the banks.

RISK TRANSFER. Companies—and, above all, SMEs—obtain required economic and financial security when they **transfer the risk of the buyer's (debtor's) default on specialized insurance company with substantial financial strength** and greater ability to use specialization and economy of scale and to cope with the risks underwritten. Insurance also helps companies in planning cash flow, guarantees their liquidity, and makes it easier to plan their business operations. Altogether, insurance has a positive impact on the credit rating of the insured companies, their credibility and reputation toward their business partners and financiers.

There is no risk-free business transaction. Due to the large risks involved with delivery on open account (clean payment), it is mainly used in short-term credits, trade between affiliated persons and, trade with unaffiliated known customers who are involved in lasting business relationships, who know each other well and have already established mutual trust. In general, such plain payment terms and conditions would not be accepted for larger business operations or long-term credits but would be applied more often for business deals with high-rated, financially strong, and experienced buyers who have excellent track records and origin from countries with trivial or low country risk. But even in these cases, it does not mean that there is no risk involved, only that the risk is kept on relatively low level. Depending on the amounts due, credit periods and various risks involved, as well as on the depth of the relationship, in such deals, creditors might seek some real or third-party security rather than conduct business on an open account basis.

The information that accounts receivable can reach up to 20–30 or even 40 percent of total company's assets is just another proof that the credit risk is really important as it can affect company's business, income statements, and balance sheets or even endanger its existence. Often accounts receivable are the single largest item in balance sheets of many companies and may frequently level with, or even exceed, capital.

Companies are bound to insure certain risk (e.g., their civil liability to third parties) and we can almost always take it for granted that they will insure their property and other assets. Why should they do otherwise with the trade receivables?

Credit insurance can adequately fulfill the needs of the companies and is therefore an essential and an integral part of their sales strategy, trade financing, and risk management. Nevertheless, a credit insurance contract can be a much better response to uncertainty or increased risk than the output adjustment. Credit insurance and auxiliary services give insurance companies a chance to offer their customers suitable and high-quality financial instruments. Through these comprehensive financial instruments, insurance companies become important providers of financing and complement the offer of other financial institutions (commercial banks, factoring companies, and other credit institutions), that support companies in their operations on domestic and foreign markets.

2.2.2 Assumption of Risk and Claims Payment
If the business is financed by the seller's, and/or external, means, he is the one who takes the risk of nonpayment unless he is properly insured

against it. After all, insurance is not free and the insurance premiums paid increase the price of goods and services or reduce the potential profit, and weaken the seller's competitive position. Depending on market position and negotiating power, sellers are often urged to credit sales and to offer open account deliveries.

●●●
_____

Insurance is a superior alternative to risk taking!
_____

The main role and function of credit insurance is the **transfer of credit risk from the insured to the insurance company**, therefore to enable safe trade and protect the seller (creditor) from nonpayment risk of its buyers (debtors).

With the conclusion of the insurance contract and by paying the insurance premium due, the insured *levels the nonpayment risk in area* and insures itself against buyers' defaults. By covering **insolvency and late payment risk**, the **liquidity risk** is reduced as well, as the policyholder's uncertain variable costs associated with debt collection transforms to fixed ones (depending on the probability of loss-causing event—considerably lower).

Risk Management Policy

The company can use numerous measures, means, and techniques as well as various legal and financial instruments to protect itself against risks, among them payment or nonpayment risk. However, companies must be familiar with protection devices and their use if they want to be successful and efficient in their business operations.

Unfortunately, there are no general recipes which tell how to successfully and efficiently protect ourselves and our companies against the risks, and likewise a principle of free enterprise does not rule *numerus clausus* of (business, financial, and legal) instruments of protection, their mode, and combination. Companies must choose instruments considering their business, capacities, risk exposure, and business goals as well as market and negotiating positions along with their admissibility, availability, and price. Equally important is the legal regulation of business relations with customers and the settlement of disputes, but it is not enough as almightiness of legal provisions and clauses might be just an illusion in the real world.

Business policy measures designed to protect against risks are not only limited to measures oriented toward risk consequences, but also toward the measures oriented to eliminate causes of loss, for example, human resource management, organizational arrangements, IT and IS development and actions that provide useful market information, planning and control over business operations, as well as risk management. All these measures and the entire process of risk management are essential and useful supplements to credit insurance and therefore important part of business policy.

Various measures of business policy or proper sales strategy and trading put companies into a position where they become very demanding toward their customers. They may impose rigorous payment terms to them and require additional securities which reduce risks or risk exposure, but on the other hand drive off or divert their existing and potential customers, thus limiting the potential market and shutting down their options for increased sales and exploitation of business opportunities. The company can try to disperse markets and buyers according to various factors (geographic and currency area, number of buyers, industry branch, etc). But due to several limitations in the competitive environment, this is rather difficult, not to mention that creating such favorable and balanced portfolios might be quite expensive and can jeopardize the exploitation of business opportunities.

COMMERCIAL RISK COVER. An **insurance policy** that obliges an insurance company to **compensate the insured through claims paid for the (financial) loss sustained**—indirect protective function or "reparation function" of credit insurance —protects the seller or exporter against the nonpayment risk of buyers due to the following commercials risks of their debtors and/or guarantors:

- Bankruptcy, liquidation, and similar events, that is, **permanent insolvency of private buyers**, and if provided by insurance policy (which is nowadays standard in credit insurance industry)
- **Protracted default**, if delivered goods are not paid in the predefined time period (typically between 90 and 180 days, but may be longer for riskier markets) after original due date of payment.

●●●
_____

Indemnification for losses is the most important ACTIVE FUNCTION OF CREDIT INSURANCE.
_____

If exports or sales deliveries are not paid on the due date or outstanding debts are not duly settled, while all conditions from the insurance policy are fulfilled, the insurer will compensate the insured (seller/creditor) for the direct material **loss** (the insurance company pays "instead of a buyer"—within the approved **credit/insurance limit** for particular buyer) at the expiration of predefined period of time (**claims waiting period**—CWP) after filing a claim/from the occurrence of the **insured event**. The "**sum insured**" (invoice value of unpaid delivery) is usually reduced by agreed **self-retention**, borne by the insured on its own account as a sort of deductible. Short-term credit insurance against commercial risks—with the aim to avoid moral hazard and to stimulate the insured to retain financial interest in preventing the occurrence of risks and recovering the part of the losses that do occur—has standard self-retention rate of 15 or 10 percent (supposed profit from transaction). Thus this insurance instrument gives the seller a possibility to efficaciously protect a bulk of his outstanding debts, that is, his open financial position to buyers as debtors who were supplied with traded goods or services on the terms of a deferred payment.

Anti-Aleatory Nature of Insurance

Insurance is not a gambling, as the property insurance consists of indemnification aspect of insurer's obligations arising from insurance contract, which indeed depends on the uncertainty of the loss-causing event. We may even talk about the anti-aleatory nature of the insurance business as well as of an individual insurance contract, as the onerous contract type. Insurance premiums paid (valuable consideration) do not only represent the payment of the insured for the compensation of the possible loss, even though the active function is the most important part of the insurance (that is, the direct purpose of the insurance), but just the mean to reach the goal—to protect the interest of the policyholder to be insured against the risks in case of occurrence of the insured event. However, the insurance premium is the compensation of the insured for the economic security gained by the insurance policy (and not a product per se). Insurance is therefore not a promise of an uncertain benefit to the insured, but the promise to compensate him for covered losses, that is, contractual and conditional personal obligation of the insurer to indemnify the insured party for loss sustained in accordance with applicable insurance conditions.

The precondition for the insurance contract is that the insured has the pecuniary interest, that is, the insured does not want the insurance event to happen and to suffer loss of property. The insured must therefore have the aim to obtain economic security through insurance (*causa securitatis*). Gambling does not have this aspect of protection against losses although the result is likewise uncertain (*l'aléa*). Economic security of the insured is the goal or purpose of the insurance contract and by no means the pleasure of the gamblers involved in game. Furthermore, the risk in credit insurance certainly does not depend much on mere coincidence as much as in gambling.

Moreover, credit insurance is an integral service, that is, next to compensation for loss sustained, the insured is also entitled to other auxiliary and supplementary services. Credit insurers may offer these auxiliary services to provide complete and comprehensive credit insurance products and services in package or separately from their basic insurance (financial) services (serviced credit insurance). The payment of insurance premiums is owed for provided insurance services and the risks underwritten (quid pro quo). In this sense then we can talk about the equality of contributions of the parties of the insurance contract. In fact, the chances for benefit are equal for both parties of the insurance contract. Policyholders pay insurance premiums, and the insurers undertake to pay larger amounts of claims equal to covered losses, if insured events occur. Otherwise the insurance is not about individual equality of contributions but a collective equality of counter-contributions of contracting parties within the "risk group," as all individual insurance contracts are by the nature and logics of insurance industry inevitably economically and financially connected. "Individual inequality" would be in favor of one of the contractual parties, depending on the loss-causing event taking place or not.

●●●──

The business practice shows that the risk of nonpayment is one of the most important risks that companies have to deal with in their business operations.

──

Credit insurance guarantees policyholders required security and gives them higher certainty to rely on planned cash flow generated through sales (credit insurance is therefore good instrument of cash management policy), provides better liquidity, and can improve creditworthiness of the insured which is important for their business partners and banks.

Because trade goods in financial markets are promises for the insurance business, it is essential that promises are kept. Without the clients' confidence in willingness and ability of insurers to pay claims for losses incurred (*damnum emergens*), the insurance would not exist at all. Being happy to sell insurance policy but reluctant to pay claims would certainly not help the widespread use of credit insurance services. Trust of the policyholders is therefore essential; otherwise credit insurers could not operate and stay on the market. The insured must have confidence in insurance companies regarding their willingness and ability to pay claims according to the insurance contract in case of occurrence of the insured event.

The security of the insured, at least from the moral point of view, also requires that the insurance conditions are sufficiently clear and unambiguous and do not include unfair or incomprehensible clauses.

●●●──

> As trust is hard to get and easy to lose, for the insurance industry it was of an utmost importance to gain the customers' trust to be able to develop to their present size.

──

Credit insurance companies are financial institutions specialized for credit risk underwriting and management. We may say that the insurer assumes the credit risk from its clients in exchange for insurance premium paid, and through dispersion transforms it into underwriting risk, that is, the risk that the insurance premium paid does not cover the claims paid and operating costs. These underwritten credit risks or technical risks burden the provisions, reserves, and equity capital of the insurance company, and may be partly or entirely transferred to the reinsurance market or even to other financial or capital markets (alternative risk transfers—ART), for example, securitization with asset-backed commercial papers (ABCP) and credit default swaps (CDS) which are also rapidly growing major substitutes for credit insurance.

Because of the nature of credit insurance, credit insurers are far more suited to assume these business risks than the sellers or exporters themselves. In principle, insurers bear the risks more easily than their clients due to the **law of large numbers**, **spreading of risks**, and the **law of probability**. Moreover, one must not forget that credit insurance companies are usually financially strong institutions. Regulators sometimes require a higher level of capital for credit insurance and, in addition to other **provisions** made against possible future losses or potential claims, credit insurers must form equalization **reserves** and manage their reserves assets with due care according to the principles of security, liquidity, and profitability. Furthermore, in heavily regulated environment, these financial institutions are licensed and bound by strict **capital adequacy requirements** and prudential supervision. Last but not least, their insurance business operations, provisioning, and investment of their assets are disclosed and under **state supervision.**

REINSURANCE. By employing reinsurance, which is also a substitute for equity, credit insurers can diversify their risk portfolio and expand their underwriting capacities. Due to the nature of the risks underwritten by credit insurers in direct insurance, and exceptionally also as joint/parallel (co-)insurance, credit insurers protect themselves against underwriting losses and cost-effectively reinsure a considerable portion of their risk portfolio, that is, passive **reinsurance**—mainly quota share treaties under which a fixed proportion of every risk is reinsured and all losses as well as all direct premiums less the reinsurance commission are shared between the ceding insurance company and reinsurer proportionately. But there are usually also several possibilities of nonproportional reinsurance, for example, surplus reinsurance or excess-loss (XL) reinsurance coverage, in the global reinsurance market with first-class reinsurers, who may cede the reinsured risks further (retrocession) and sometimes also transfer them to capital markets.

Companies with insured sales (accounts receivable) are seen as trustworthy from the suppliers' point of view, which means that they might negotiate better payment terms and conditions, sales on credit or deferred payment terms without requested securities as well as higher credit limits for their deliveries. Furthermore, they may even obtain favorable financing conditions from banks and other financial institutions.

With the duration of a transaction generally, the risk is growing and the uncertainty increases because the predictability is worsening with the prolongation of term.

International trade companies encounter similar risks as in the domestic market. However, **risks in international trade are generally larger and of a specific type**. They may also reflect in different ways as in the domestic market. There are various economic and legal regulations and practice in the world influenced by different factors, for example, remote markets, various means of transportation and more participants, longer crediting period, larger business volume, stronger competition, infrequent acquaintance between seller and buyer, as well as political and other noncommercial risks involved in international trade.

As mentioned before, the risk is future, uncertain event causing financial loss providing that the company is not insured against such risk.

Next to the above insurance conditions—which may seem logical, but are in practice and in some cases somehow incomprehensible for the insureds who must prove their legally valid interest in the insurance—**the insured risk must be possible and independent of the insurance contract parties' (exclusive) will, which is one of the basic insurance principles. Insurance involves outside risk, and an insured party that causes the occurrence of an insured event intentionally or by gross negligence will not get the claims paid.**

To be able to talk about the risk underwritten by the insurance company with its negative and positive starting constant, the loss-causing event must be possible, and absolutely or at least relatively uncertain (*l'aléa*) and must take place in the future—the insurance domain is normally the future, not the past or present.

Otherwise, an insurer is obliged to cover accounts receivable that have come into existence after the conclusion of the insurance contract or after the date stipulated in the insurance contract as the start of the insurance coverage, as well as the accounts receivable that arose before these dates, but only on the condition that they were not due before these dates. Such overdue trade receivables can only be transferred to debt collecting agencies at big discounts.

Existing risk is a precondition for an insurance contract. The insured has business intentions and beneficial interest to protect himself from existing risks; however, the consequences of occurrence of these risks (loss-causing events) must not be foreseen and, as a rule, at a future time from when the insurance contract has been concluded. If the insurance covers the event that had already occurred, *causa* for the insurance contract would normally be missing; in such a case, there is no risk anymore, but only certainty that the risk will be (was) brought into effect. The loss-causing event must therefore be uncertain—we can talk about existential and sometimes even time-dependent or quantitative risk components—although underwriters and actuaries estimate the likelihood and extent of probable losses as well as the time of their occurrence. As an example, an insurance company would not insure an already burning house, because there is a certainty of damage, that is, the probability of loss-causing event is 100 percent. Likewise, the insurance contract would most likely be null and void if someone wanted to insure the fish in a fish farm against fire. The insurance domain is therefore probability expressed in mathematical form as a value between 0 and 1—in other words, the area between impossibility and necessity. However, it is very difficult to predict a particular loss-causing event in credit insurance as well as in other insurance classes; past performance, for example, is not always a guide to future performance. On the other hand, due to the law of probability, along with risk dispersion, the predictability of loss-causing events is certainly increased at large volume of business insured.

Painful experiences from companies demonstrate that the payment discipline in several countries, more or less promising industries, as well as of business partners is not exactly something to be praised. Unfortunately, this is not true for underdeveloped countries only, but for developed and successful economies as well. Solvency problems are not rare phenomena and no company is immune.

Commercial and noncommercial risks

- **Nonpayment risk** or risk of delayed payment unfortunately occurs quite frequently in domestic and foreign markets. These risks are a usual source of bitter experiences. More or less subjective reasons drive debtors to cause these risks. When we talk about **commercial risks**—the risk related to the private buyer and debtor or guarantor and their willingness and/or ability to pay, it is mostly the buyer's (debtor's) inability to pay (default), either due to his (i) **permanent insolvency** (bankruptcy, winding-up, or similar events) or (ii) an **extended payment delay**, for example, 6 monthly **protracted default**, or sometimes even avoidance or rescission of a contract or any other fundamental breach of contract caused by the buyer, such as his inability to take over delivered goods and/or shipping documents.

- Loss caused to the seller by the buyer's default can be material or immaterial, total or partial, and it may sometimes be recovered at a later stage with or without extra costs. Due to nonpayment of overdue debts, the seller may face not only special **recovery risk**, but also some additional risks, for example, procedural or **legal risks** and costs.

These risks can be a reflection of the buyer's moral values and bad business habits which usually influence his business reputation and reliability toward his business partners and banks. The main attribute of these risks is that the buyer (debtor) is not willing to fulfill his obligations or does not want to fulfill them in the manner agreed upon, that is, with due care and diligence.

Even more frequently, these "firm-specific" business risks occur without the buyer's will or even against his will. If the insurance covers **COMMERCIAL RISKS** of nonpayment, the reason for nonperformance must be under the control of the private debtor or at least within his sphere.

There are many reasons for buyers' default. However, internal and external reasons for payment incapability of debtors are often interlaced. Even trustworthy and well-run companies can be affected by various adverse trends and events over which they have little control. Several analyses of companies' downfalls show that there are numerous and often hardly predictable reasons for misfortunes and bankruptcies:

- Poor management
- High overheads
- Overambitious plans, excessive business volume, investments, etc.
- Inadequate financial control
- Bad buyers, irregular or missed payments, and collapse of the key customers
- Inefficient debt collection
- Unfavorable cash flow, not brought in line with company's liabilities
- High inflation or unfavorable exchange rates and other market risk
- Reduced demand, economic recession, and worsening of terms of trade
- Natural and other catastrophes
- Inappropriate or late response to market changes, etc.

• Next to the "micro" risks mentioned above, international trade may be exposed to various country- and global-specific **political** and other **NONCOMMERCIAL RISKS**. These "macro" risks can be underwritten by ECAs and other credit insurers separately or in a combination package together with the commercial risks, considering the riskiness of doing business, the type of risk, the risk horizon, the debtor's status (public or private buyer/guarantor), and its geographic location.

Private insurers normally underwrite the above risks that affect the companies only in combination with commercial risk coverage, if they are capable and willing to bear them. If the private (reinsurance) market generally does not take account on the risks due to their nature, location, size—large lumps and risk horizon, unpredictability, accumulation of risks, unbalanced portfolio, poor dispersion and legal insecurity, or due to difficult prevention of loss-causing events or recoveries, etc., they are perceived as **nonmarketable risks**, which remain in the domain of national ECAs dealing with officially supported export credit insurance in the interest of the national economies. While capacity of the private (re) insurance market varies, the definition of (non-)marketable risks is not immutable and changes over time (see, for example, *Communication of the Commission to the Member States pursuant to Article 93 (1) of the EC*

Treaty applying Articles 92 and 93 of the Treaty to short-term export-credit insurance—97/C 281/03 (OJ C 281, 17. 9. 1997) with its amendments).

Export Credit Agencies

Raison d'être. Due to favorable macroeconomic effects and possible other national interests and because of the nature of nonmarketable risks and to fill market gaps and alleviate market failures—for example, unapplied actuarial statistics, high unpredictability of the political risks, their catastrophic and systemic nature, concentration of risk portfolio, and possible accumulation of losses—almost all developed and many underdeveloped countries use tools of their foreign trade policy to stimulate exports by complementing private market and insuring export credits against noncommercial and commercial risks **(second best solution)** through their officially supported ECAs, bearing in mind required transparency, *acquis communautaire*, and their break-even objective over the long term and the ban on export subsidies imposed within the framework of World Trade Organization (WTO) regulations or agreed international rules and guidelines on export credits (OECD "Consensus"—Arrangement on Officially Supported Export Credits), respectively.

Insurance facilities. ECAs, carrying full faith and credit of their respective governments, commonly do not cover domestic trade and are primarily concerned with one-off medium-term export credits in national interest. Here we talk about "tied financing," as the United States are not very eager to finance or insure the exports of other countries on the burden of national budgets and their taxpayers. Next to insuring export credits in the narrow sense, especially with the maturities of more than 2 years, many ECAs with the backing of their governments insure Foreign Outward Direct Investments against noncommercial risks and bank guarantees against unfair calling risk or fair calling of guarantees due to noncommercial risks. Furthermore, they may provide insurance cover for construction equipment and material, consignment goods, or exhibited goods in exhibitions and fairs held or taking place abroad against political risks. Certain export transactions and direct investments may also be insured against exchange rate risks, etc.

Some larger private credit insurance companies offer coverage also for longer-term transactions, they provide insurance of FDIs and bank guarantees, and some of them insure medium-term credits against commercial as well as noncommercial risks, sometimes even with a maturity of up to 5 years or more.

Indirect or **direct political risks** and **risks of natural catastrophes** are rather heterogeneous and are accessory to commercial risks. Political risks relate to various extraordinary and adverse events or circumstances all of which need not, however, have a political background, that may arise in the debtor's country or in connection with its country preventing the buyer or his guarantor from paying or to transfer the amount due to the exporter's country. They are largely exogenous to the exporters and mostly external, that is, they are usually not related to business manners or behavior of private debtors but to economic crises, wars and warlike events, governmental measures and administrative actions, natural disasters, etc. Reasons for their occurrences are mostly objective, beyond the influence of buyer and seller and can also be **systemic risks**, which means that they can affect all subjects doing business in a particular country (accumulation of losses). Often they are presented to the contracting parties as an **act of God** (*force majeure/vis maior*). Contracting parties cannot apply actuarial models and cannot foresee loss-causing events in case of noncommercial risks or otherwise have difficulties predicting and preventing them as well as their consequences. In case of political or noncommercial risk cover, payment default or contract nonexecution actually cannot be prevented and direct consequences of such events are the exporters' losses. By the insured events, the payment or another performance must be prevented, at least partly, and the insured exporter must suffer material loss as a result.

Nonexhaustive list of the **noncommercial risks**:

- **Nonpayment and revoking** or **contract frustration by sovereign states and various public buyers and/or guarantors**
- **War, insurrection, riots, general strikes** (with clear political purpose) and other **civil disturbances**
- **Confiscation, expropriation**, and **nationalization** (CEN)
- **Import/export restrictions**, including **embargoes**
- **General moratorium** on repayment of external debt
- **Debt write-off, rescheduling**, or **restructuring**
- Risk of local currency **conversion** into hard (convertible and freely transferable) currency and/or its **transfer** abroad **(convertibility risk)**
- Other **currency** and **exchange rate risks** including market **interest rate risks**
- **Catastrophic risks**—risks of natural catastrophes such as floods, volcanic eruption, earthquake, hurricane, and tidal waves.

As we can see, international trade is prone to numerous perils beyond the control of the supplier and its buyer. Commercial and political risks are interrelated to some extent. Economic cycles, political upheavals, and changes in regulations may affect all firms and create uncertainty and possibility for damages and interruption of trade and financial flows. They may lead to interruption or changes in contractual relations or may prevent a buyer from paying for delivered goods and rendered services. Such risks are undoubtedly bigger (the biggest risk is usually one we do not see coming) in underdeveloped or politically unstable countries. However, they do exist in developed countries as well—terrorism, regulation changes, for example, environmental, veterinarian, and phyto-sanitary, but might be trivial.

BLURRED DISTINCTION BETWEEN COMMERCIAL AND NONCOMMERCIAL RISKS. The **distinction between commercial and noncommercial risks has become blurred** and these risks are sometimes difficult to distinguish in practice. According to the **doctrine of proximate cause of loss**, noncommercial risks as remote causes of loss (*causa remota*) can result in occurrence of commercial risks. For this reason, it may be **useful for the insured to make a package insurance contract covering not only commercial, but also political and other noncommercial risks, that is, comprehensive insurance cover** that can be available under a single "umbrella" insurance policy and tailored to meet particular needs and external circumstances. For many international trade deals, especially those of a larger size, longer credit terms, large or unique cargoes or buyers, and guarantors located in distant and high-risk emerging markets, it might be advisable for the creditors to take out also political risk insurance.

In contemporary trade, also the boundaries between export and domestic sales are becoming blurred or even erased due to globalization. Similarly, the distinction between commercial and noncommercial risks may be blurred because several different direct and indirect causes for default may be interlaced. Nowadays, insurance policies are therefore often combined, insuring export as well as domestic sales against commercial and noncommercial risks **(global whole turnover insurance policies with comprehensive coverage)**.

Insurance against nonpayment risks creates potential for growth, helps companies to increase sales as well as to ensure their competitive position on the market. Companies can use credit insurance to offer their customers favorable and safe credit sales under competitive terms and conditions.

By transferring payment risks to insurance companies, sellers get the opportunity to offer their customers not only merchandise, but also competitive payment terms and financing, because they can be certain that the debt payment or repayment of credit will take place. Credit insurance therefore helps vendors to provide competitive offers compared to other suppliers who are not able to offer such sales and payment terms, thus keeping the existing customers and increasing sales volume, as well as penetrating into higher-risk markets and spreading their presence to new markets and customers.

Domestic and Export Credit Insurance

Commercial risks of payment defaults are more or less frequent in any market economy and above all amidst unstable economic conditions and poor payment discipline; however, in exports, the risks are in general even greater and are expressed in a different way. It is often far more difficult to export as it is to sell on the domestic market, because for the exporters the variety and extent of unforeseen loss-causing events are usually much greater than for the companies dealing with the trade on their local and well-known markets.

International trade may be exposed to additional risks and have the following characteristics:

— Remoteness of markets
— Insufficient knowledge on business partners
— Larger number of participants, that is, forwarding agents, transport and insurance companies, banks, and state authorities
— Different climate
— Longer and multimodal transportation
— Financing on longer credit as well as longer and more rigorous payment terms and conditions
— Inadequate and less up-to-date credit information
— Different economic, political and legal systems, and other political factors
— Different business customs, language, and culture
— Trade barriers
— Various currencies and monetary systems
— Foreign exchange control
— Stronger competition
— Larger volume of international business, etc.

Credit insurance can be a useful tool for companies to be insured against nonpayment risk, especially in export transactions where it is usually more difficult to assess and monitor the debtors' risks and to enforce overdue payments. On the other hand, as mentioned before, globalization and internationalization of companies erases boundaries between domestic sales and exports. Intra-group trade is gaining momentum—it even prevails in international trade. Companies keep asking for insurance cover for trade on domestic and all export markets. Therefore, the insurers discern less and less between insurance of export or domestic credits, while at the same time, there is a growing trend of insurance policies that cover the nonpayment risks of all customers of the insured company, that is, **global insurance policies** covering the **whole turnover** of the insured.

2.2.3 Preventive Function of Credit Insurance

●●●————————————————————————————————————

Credit insurance provides the sellers strong financial and other protection and transfers the risk of nonpayment to the insurance company specialized in credit insurance and capable of bearing this risk.

——

Due to economy of scale, specialization and know-how as well as the law of large numbers, the dispersion of risks—insurance is always grounded on the principle of mutuality and solidarity—financial strength, capital base, and reinsurance arrangements (insurance companies act as a sort of "broker" between the insured and the reinsurance companies), insurers are definitely better equipped to bear these risks than any particular company. Companies are oriented toward narrow market segments and limited number of geographically separated markets. They often cannot afford to invest in collecting country, industrial sector, or company-specific information as well as in processing required data and performing activities required to prevent or minimize losses. Such expenses on internal information system (IS) costs definitely increase with the heterogeneity of the sellers' customer base and their different geographic locations.

It is not always easy for an individual company and can be time consuming and expensive to obtain quality information on customers, primarily about the prospective and targeted new ones. The task is even more difficult, as many companies successfully hide compromising information from their partners and may try to solve problems at the expense of their creditors. The reliability of the customer meant as willingness and ability of the debtor to fulfill his obligations is therefore of key importance for sellers (creditors). Unfortunately, the insolvency of the buyers may come totally unexpectedly and often catch suppliers by surprise. Bankruptcies do not only happen in times of recession (depending on the elasticity of the demand, some branches may be more affected then others) but also in times of recovery, because increased competition may increase the problems of companies, which can lead them into bankruptcy.

CREDIT INFORMATION. Credit information on buyers is therefore very important for the creditors, especially if they sell on open account. This information is equally important to the insurers in taking over those risks from companies and managing them. One of the most important pieces of credit information for companies and lenders is the **credit rating** of their debtors, because it shows their creditworthiness also in comparison with other companies. The analysis is oriented toward the estimation of likelihood that the company will not go bankrupt, along with probability and its ability to pay debts by using evaluation of the trends and forecasts including established **credit limit**, that is, a credit recommendation regarding suggested payment terms and conditions as well as about the limit amount up to which the buyer can be safely credited without additional securities.

Firstly, for credit information, the companies may request formal banker's references (bearing in mind banking secrecy and the bank's duty of discretion to its clients), but these references are rather vague in practice. There are also numerous mercantile agents and some global **credit rating agencies** with online services such as, for example, Dun & Bradstreet, which issue more or less detailed **credit reports** on the basis of global data basis information on numerous companies from almost all countries and with their presence on local markets. Static and dynamic analysis of financial data from debtor's annual reports for the last few years is undoubtedly important for credit reports. However, this is mostly *ex post* data, which is not always accurate, updated, or credible, but is, nevertheless, the only more or less objective basis for assessment and estimation of *ex ante* liquidity and creditworthiness of buyers, that is, the probability that buyers will settle their debts at their maturity, for the payment terms and the credit amount approved.

Country-risk assessments and reports play an important role in international business too. These risk assessments and such composite risk indicators combine and summarize different political, macroeconomical, and financial risks that are generally in connection with commercial and financial operations taking place in a particular country and certain period of time. A country-risk assessment is not always very reliable prediction of future situation and trends, but nevertheless, country-risk reports provide companies and financial institutions with useful information on their business environment. Reliability of assessment not only depends on quality and accuracy of information, but also on timely horizon of forecasts, different quantitative and qualitative methods and their combinations, and number and importance of utilized indicators.

INFORMATION CAPITAL. An insurance company specialized in credit risk insurance must be proficient in identifying and estimating these risks. Basic components of credit insurance products are in fact information, and there is always a certain amount of art as well as experience that is required in credit risk assessment. Therefore, experience and information capital, a highly developed IS and an extensive database of quality and accurate data and information, including "soft information," gathered from internal as well as primary and secondary external sources worldwide are of vital importance. This information makes the insurer to be well acquainted with the risks underwritten, that is, with the buyers and their industries as well as with the broader economic, political, and legal environment. Quality and up-to-date information and subjective experiences (underwriting flair) are very important for credit insurance, although this type of insurance is sometimes considered more art than science, meaning it requires long years of practical experience and "feeling."

●●●
___

To prevent danger is always better than to cure its harmful consequences.
___

Information gathered by insurance companies about country-risk and creditworthiness of existing and potential buyers is vitally important for successful marketing, sales, and business success. It forms and contributes to the **PREVENTIVE FUNCTION OF CREDIT INSURANCE.**

●●●
___

Praestat cautela quam medela.
___

OBLIGATIONS TO REPORT. Insured party is obliged to provide its credit insurer information regarding all important circumstances that may influence the risks, for example, delayed payments, if it was informed about these circumstances during the business with the customer, or it should be familiar with them by acting with due diligence. Credit insurance contract is a contract *uberrimae fidei*. Therefore, according to insurance conditions, the insured is obliged to disclose all material facts and to inform the insurance company in (utmost) good faith. This is an essential contractual obligation of the insured. The sanction for non-performance may be a withdrawal from contract or even refusal or reduction of the claims paid; that means the insurer can "avoid" the policy. Furthermore, the insurer has access to numerous other options for gathering information—even those that are not accessible to public.

According to an insurance contract, the insured is obliged to fill out in good faith and with due care the **application form—request for insurance** with the detailed **questionnaire**. Along with other data, the insured should list his buyers and describes his trading history and business experience, for example, annual turnover, payment terms and conditions, eventual payment delays, and frequency. Relations between the seller and the buyer have an important influence on risk assessment. In his request, the insured estimates the volume of trade (credits) for each customer, the average payment terms, and conditions. Accordingly, in its **request for approval/increase of debtor's insurance limit,** the insured proposes the amount of insurance (credit) limits of his buyers. Credit information on the debtor may be attached to the request.

The insured must act according to the principle of civil law of good faith as well as promptly, fully, and fairly report to the insurance company all material facts and relevant circumstances of which he is aware of (or should be aware of as a good manager in the ordinary course of business) if they may influence the risk assessment and the conclusion (and alteration or termination) of the insurance contract, as well as insurance conditions, for example, insurance premium rate and insurance limits (see for authoritative definition of "material facts and circumstances," for example, *Container Transport International Inc. v. Oceanus Mutual Underwriting Association (Bermuda) Ltd. (1984) 1 Lloyd's Rep. 476* and *Pan Atlantic Insurance Co. Ltd. and Another v. Pine Top Insurance Co. Ltd. (1994) CL 379*). By no means may the insured deliberately make a misrepresentation, nondisclosure or false disclosure, or conceal circumstances that might result in the judgement of a prudent underwriter (note: the attitude of the actual insurer is thus not a criterion) not to refuse cover or to offer insurance coverage under less stringent conditions (note: it is not necessary to prove that the insurer actual decision would have been different). It might even be regarded as insurance fraud. Even negligence in duty of accurate disclosure and reporting, or the breach of obligation to report about the circumstances that may influence the risk, can be a valid reason for an insurer to impose sanctions against the insured. One can also frequently find specific provisions inserted in credit insurance conditions with regard to duties of disclosure and the accuracy of the information requested and provided which contain subtle distinctions from the general civil and common law principles. This is one important big difference of credit insurance contract (*differentia specifica*) that distinguishes it from other commercial and insurance contracts.

According to the principle of good faith, the insured is <u>obliged to update given information and to keep the insurance company informed about all relevant circumstances and changed circumstances he became aware of after the conclusion of the insurance contract</u> or during the implementation of the insurance contract if they influence the risk, increase the probability of its occurrence or the size of potential loss. If the circumstances and buyer's risk change after the conclusion of the insurance contract, for example, actual or imminent insolvency of the buyer, the insured is obliged to submit the required specific information. In case of omission, according to general insurance conditions, the coverage for credits extended to a particular debtor may be revoked or become void. If the insured fails to fulfill his obligations, the insurer may refuse to pay the claim, and if the infringement is serious or repeated, it may even cancel the contract (*ultima ratio*). This is, of course, not the case in suretyship; the liability of the issuer of the surety bond and the rights of the obligees are not affected by misrepresentation by the applicant (principal).

The sanctions are pretty rigorous and depend on the gravity of the infringement or breach. The burden of proof about the omission or false disclosure and reporting, fraud and on the consecutive damage rests with the insurer. Such on the first sight rigorous sanctions stipulated in insurance contracts are legitimate because otherwise the insurer may be mislead toward mistakenly covering high-risk debtors, while the responsibility of the insured for causing or increasing the loss sustained is very hard to prove due to **asymmetry of information**. Often sellers have close-knitted relationships and experience in long-term business cooperation with their buyers, thus they get to know their customers (risks) better than an insurance company. Another reason for rather rigorous sanctions is the existence of the **moral hazard** mentioned before and the nature of underwritten commercial credit risks. For the above reasons, the contracting sanctions foreseen for not performing the reporting duty are understandable and stringent necessity, but are rarely seen in general insurance conditions of other types of property insurance.

An insurance contract provides a company indirect access to information on buyers, their financials and companies' specific behavior on payments of their debts, which is disclosed to insurers also by other clients. The most important information assessed by the insurance company is the data about latest available financials, insolvency procedures, payment discipline of the buyers, recorded payment delays or defaults, information on business habits and problems the companies are confronting on a particular market or within a particular industry branch, etc.

Furthermore, in addition to a wide range of credit information from their own business experience, insurance companies have access to various credit information provided by specialized business operators and credit agencies, banks, factors, and other financial institutions and chambers of commerce. For instance, a buyer can have an account at several banks and use other bank services. Certainly credit insurance companies do not rely on information from a single credit agency, but may search for a second, third, etc. opinion on creditworthiness of a particular buyer.

The prices for credit information, made available to the insured **through his credit insurer**, may be **lower** due to volume of orders. Credit information and risk monitoring as auxiliary services can also be a part of the integral insurance package offered—serviced credit insurance.

Furthermore, credit insurer or ECA in particular has an access to other public sources, diplomatic channels and sources that are normally not available to public. This is primarily the important information shared by the insurer with its reinsurers and other primary insurers, for example, *via* international associations such as ICISA or Berne Union.

Enterprises and insurance companies conclude an insurance contract and agree about the buyers that will be insured and their **insurance limits**. Insurers do not insure nonpayment risk of all customers, for example, buyers with an inadequate credit rating, and credit insurance cover cannot be granted unless there is a reasonable probability that the debt will be repaid at due date or within short period thereafter. The risk underwritten should be a sound one, meaning that the buyer is not likely to have problems with its debts. Occasionally, an exception is negative vetting—simplified handling of "automatic" or other smaller insurance limits when the insured has only positive experience with payments of a particular buyer and in general there is no negative information about the buyer. For credit insured sellers, it is easier to get in business deals and to take risks, as credit insurance enlightens the distinction and choice between good and bad risks. With the help of insurer, enterprises may therefore assess the creditworthiness of their buyers more easily and cheaper, and can find it easier to decide which customers can purchase on the deferred payment terms as well as to choose the amount of the supplier credits and define their terms and conditions.

This preventive function of credit insurance is valuable to companies, because it **helps them to create the concept and implementation method of their business and sales strategy as well as their credit policy** (sales volume on deferred payment terms/outstanding debts—credit limits, amounts, currencies, payment terms and instruments, etc.).

Relying on internal risk management or risk mitigation is almost impossible or at least suboptimal for many enterprises. Certainly, the transfer of financial (credit) risks to the insurance company not only brings more efficient risk management, but also helps to reduce costs. The benefits of the credit insurance may decisively surpass the expenses for insurance.

INSURANCE LIMITS. When companies have established business cooperation with their customers, paying their debts without significant delay and the trade receivables represent relatively small amounts, the insurer underwrites the risk of these particular buyers to a certain "automatic limits," for example, EUR 15,000 or 25,000, without additional checking of their creditworthiness. Limit of such insurance coverage is a total amount of cumulative outstanding debts of a particular debtor, which are "automatically" taken over on the grounds of insurance declaration only (monthly list of commercial invoices). For given buyers, **discretionary limits** can be approved to experienced clients up to the maximum discretionary limit, setting by the insureds themselves on the basis of available accurate credit information and/or their good trading experience. Other buyers are accepted in the insurance only if their rating is adequate and for the credits which may not exceed allocated insurance (credit) limits; the accounts receivable surpassing these limits because of the increased sales volume will not be covered, but the policyholder is obliged to report to the insurer such increased sales volume anyway. If the approved limits are not sufficient, the insured may request their increase; such increase, if approved, may be temporary, for instance, to cover seasonal supplies.

Insurance will be refused for buyers whose creditworthiness is not adequate. For such buyers, the insurer may suggest and require collateral, for example, besides customary retention of title (ROT), the insurer can also demand additional securities, comfort letters, or guarantees of mother companies and third persons.

RISK MONITORING. Credit insurers continuously, or from time to time—for example, regularly on a yearly basis, monitor economic conditions for particular markets and industries, and perform **risk monitoring**. In fact, local insurers and in early stages of internationalization credit insurers mainly monitored the domestic companies and exchanged credit information when insuring export credits. Based on the monitoring results of checking whether financial position of the buyers have not deteriorated after the approval of insurance limits, as well as according to the needs of the insured to cover the increased sales volume, an insurer may define a different insurance limit for an individual buyer, larger or smaller, compared to the original limit. We can describe insurance limits as being "alive" because they are constantly managed by credit insurer, thus managing their credit risk exposure. The credit **migration (deterioration/downgrade) risk**, that is, the risk that the credit rating of the debtor may deteriorate over time, is always present. In lifetime of the insurance contract, the insurer is therefore entitled to impose other limitations and more rigorous insurance conditions, that is, shorter payment terms, ROT, and other real and personal securities, and may impose other measures for reduction of risk, improvement of possibilities for debt collection, and subsequent recoveries of the claims paid as well. Furthermore, on the basis of risk monitoring, warning signs of slow payment reports or deteriorating balance sheet, the insurer may revoke the cover for new credits to a particular buyer or all buyers from a particular country; however, the insured must receive (written) notice about this measure. On the basis of improved credit rating of the buyer, the insurer may also decide to subsequently include the credits extended to buyers that were previously not covered. The alterations of insurance coverage can only be arranged for future claims; of course, existing transactions and trade receivables remain fully covered by the insurance contract with unchanged insurance conditions.

Cooperation with an insurance company gives an enterprise access to quality and up-to-date information about customers (early warnings) that was already in the insurer's possession before the underlying commercial contract was concluded and allows access to this information during the whole time that cooperation with foreign or domestic buyers takes place. If the circumstances change, the insurer will normally immediately inform the insured, thus giving him opportunity to adjust his sales strategy as well as credit policy and business plans on the basis of information shared with the insurance company.

Quantitative and qualitative information on customers, including soft information from credit insurers, is sometimes even more important than financial analysis based on the *ex post* data. It offers additional comfort to managers responsible for credits, risks, and finance. At the same time, this information enables them to be proactive toward sales departments and indicates fields in which the company has better chances for success. In case the insurer is able to quickly provide information and approve buyers' credit limits, it enables companies bound by "just-in-time deliveries" to rapidly adjust their sales policy and payment terms thus challenging new business opportunities.

Credit insurance and accompanying services are therefore important instruments of risk management that help companies to run efficacious sales and crediting policy. Credit insurance services enable sellers to select appropriate payment terms and conditions as well as to establish credit limits for their buyers and to perform risk monitoring with the aim to adjust their business according to changes in buyers' creditworthiness and other circumstances.

Information on buyers and their economic environment provided by the insurance companies is essential and very useful for risk management and business plans of enterprises, but cannot be completely substituted by credit insurance policy alone.

If credit insurer refuses to insure a particular buyer, this may be the biggest financial benefit to the insured. It would prevent the time and costs wasted on an account which would never be paid. In such a case, it is definitely not wise to enter into business without additional securities. Companies can thus avoid high probability of payment default and painful losses. It may even happen that some companies try to insure their deliveries to nonexisting buyers or buyers that have not paid their overdue debts.

Most often, buyers do not owe only one supplier—their debts may be cumulated with debts to other sellers or creditors. Excessive accumulation of debts may lead to bankruptcy, which may occasionally, and in some locations quite frequently, be intentional—with a goal of unjust enrichment and creditor impairment.

Even the information on approved insurance limits alone may be useful to companies, as they reflect the financial capability of buyers and their ability to pay their debts in due time. These limits, set by credit insurers as a part of the credit recommendation, are by all means taken "more seriously" than credit reports and recommendations by other credit rating agencies which merely provide their professional opinions, as they are not just the reflection of the buyer's payment record and the debtor's credit rating, but are also backed up by the insurer, which is willing to bear the default risk of a particular buyer up to the predefined limit. In other words, insurer will bear the risk and not merely gives its opinion to the company, letting it take all the risk by itself.

The set insurance limits do not reflect only the buyer's credit rating, but may, on the other hand, reflect also their utilization and exposure of the insurer against the debtor, its capacities and the limits set for the primary insurer by the reinsurers. The assessment of creditworthiness in order to approve a certain credit must therefore take into consideration these factors as well. Credit insurer may divide, for instance, the buyer's aggregate (cumulative) limit among several other insured parties.

Credit information available to insurers is therefore valuable for the companies, their sales policy, and risk management, even if some of their buyers are not included in the insurance contract for various reasons.

2.2.4 Prevention of Claims, Their Minimization, and Recoveries
The importance of credit insurance is not limited to claims payment that compensates the insured for the damage caused by payment default (active function of insurance) and proven improvement of credit risk

management enabled by the excellent IT support and consulting services of credit insurance companies, but also offers additional **prevention and reducing of losses** by the **CURATIVE AND REPRESSIVE FUNCTION OF CREDIT INSURANCE.**

Damages to the property of sellers may be incurred on the basis of loss-causing events that lead to, according to applicable insurance conditions, the occurrence of **insured event**, that is, nonpayment due to insolvency or protracted default. For many companies, extended payment delays may be an even greater problem than the bankruptcies of their buyers, which can threaten even the most solid companies.

DISCREET NATURE. Buyers are usually not familiar with the fact that their debts are insured; at least until their credit insurance limits are significantly reduced or canceled. Such knowledge may even increase **moral hazard** when buyer and seller both know that the unpaid debt will be compensated for by the insurer; therefore, they would probably not put much effort into payment or debt collection. Credit insurance contracts and their contents are normally confidential as well as set or refused credit insurance limits which may be in insurance conditions explicitly treated as confidential information. We are referring to the "**discretion of credit insurance**," that is, the insurance company is most often "silent" business and financial partner of the insured creditor. However, the cooperation with an insurance company mostly reduces the risk of payment default associated with the business transaction.

IMPACTS. Credit insurance may have a significant influence on better payment discipline, may stimulate enterprises to give consideration to payment terms and conditions, and may, in general, help to create better business ethics. When dealing with debtors who do not fulfill their obligations, an insurance company may also utilize nonlegal sanctions, which are sometimes even more efficient than legal sanctions and actions arising from the underlying commercial contracts and applicable laws.

For the debtor, the insurance company may be significantly more important than the single vendor. Therefore, its inclusion in the business transaction guarantees consideration of payment terms and conditions agreed upon, as well as reduces the likelihood of nonpayment. It may also reduce **legal risks** by granting the insured company (creditor) better chances for **debt collection** and consecutive **recoveries** of the claims paid.

The insurer is not dependent on the buyer and its business co-operation to the same extent as the seller who wants to keep "good business relationships" or even increase the volume of business. Debtors who are late with payments may often avoid contacts with creditors. If the debtor is harping on the seller's interest in further business cooperation when debt collection takes place, the seller can use the pressure of the credit insurer and his demands as an excuse to collect his debts and to be able to proceed with deliveries. Direct involvement of the credit insurer in the debt collection furthermore disburdens the company from "unpleasant" activities which may lead to resentment and make further cooperation between the partners impossible or at least difficult.

Moreover, experience and poor payment discipline of a buyer involved in credit insurance may also influence his reputation and the volume of credits he can obtain from other suppliers or financial institutions. The credits of other suppliers can be insured for the same buyer.

- Along with other data, credit insurers often exchange the information on pending claims, claims under consideration, as well as data on claims paid, credit rating, and payment discipline of buyers. If the insured credit is not repaid on the due date, that information may be easily spread to a wide circle of the buyer's existing and potential business partners. This may significantly affect his business reputation ("intangible" **reputation risk**), thus limiting or closing his access to various financial and other business opportunities.
- Companies are well aware that credit insurance companies have several possibilities as well as successful **legal and claims departments** to cooperate with specialized **debt collection agencies** who better know the particular markets, customs and legal rules, and procedures. Credit insurers have also established successful cooperation in debt collection and recoveries. It is particularly difficult for companies to collect their debts in foreign markets by themselves, especially in insolvency proceedings, because detailed knowledge on national regulations, local customs, and business practice is required. Successful debt collection often requires fast actions and services of arranged experienced local debt collectors and lawyers.

* It is well known that debt collection is much more successful if activities and procedures are started as soon as possible. By all means, one should react if the payment delay exceeds the customary time period for a particular buyer or market. The buyer's counter-claims must also be dealt with promptly. Therefore, it is **important to inform the insurer, on a regular basis and promptly, about any unusual or excessive payment delay** of a particular buyer (note on payment delays) or about the **circumstances which lead to or may lead to payment default** and occurrence of an insured event.

As already stated, in accordance with general insurance conditions, the **insured is obliged to pay attention and to consider the instructions of the insurer regarding the measures required to prevent the loss-causing events and to minimize their consequences.** According to applicable insurance conditions, the insured is obliged to keep the amount of its outstanding accounts receivable to a particular buyer within the approved insurance limit (**prohibition of "overloading/overtrading"**). If the payment delay exceeds the usually tolerated limit of 30 days and sometimes even more, the insured must not increase his exposure to an unreliable buyer and has to stop further supplies immediately. He must also take all other practicable measures and activities to prevent and minimize the loss, for example, to initiate legal or out-of-court procedures.

Credit insurer should be informed by the insured of all material facts and circumstances important from the point of risk. Thus, the insurer will be able to better assist companies in fast and efficient debt collection. If this is not feasible, companies will be indemnified by the claims paid.

Debt collection, which may be an additional and special outsourced service as part of **serviced credit insurance**, is due to specialization of the credit insurer and his professional experience and international connections with other insurers, banks, lawyers, and debt collecting agencies, significantly **relieved** and **improved**, and often even **cheaper** for the company. Along with fixed **handling fees**, which are usually charged on a success-fee basis, the debt collection costs depend mostly on the outstanding amounts, their age, the debtor's country, and the volume of business being trusted to the insurer.

Debt collection procedures require close cooperation between insurers and insured parties. The insurers act firmly but courteously and pay special attention to the interest of the insured creditors that are still in business with their buyers. Normally the collection activities take their course on the basis of an agreement made between the parties of an insurance contract, where the insured may suggest to the insurance company how aggressively it should collect the debts.

Along with debt collection, some credit insurers and other financial institutions offer companies other packages or comprehensive services of debt management, including debt buyback and debt swaps.

The costs of measures for loss prevention or minimization are shared between the insured and the insurer, irrespective of the success of the above measures. The share of the expenses borne by the insurer is, in general, equal to the percentage of insurance coverage, that is, the larger part of the costs is borne by the insurance company. However, loss prevention activities of the insured along with costs arising from these measures must be founded and reasonably incurred. With the exception of urgent cases, the insured must get **approval of the insurer** before the measures are taken.

Even after the claim is already paid, insurers often succeed in loss recoveries, that is, they recover larger or smaller shares of outstanding debt amount—**recoveries**. Recoveries are, in addition to premium paid, unlike in some other insurance types, very important income for credit insurers, and they are usually lower in insolvency proceedings (e.g., 5 percent in bankruptcies and 50 percent in successful rehabilitation) and higher when the claim is paid for protracted default where the amount of the claim paid can be recovered in full. According to the insured's **self-retention percentage** stated in the insurance contract, the later recoveries are split between the insurer and the insured *pro rata*, which means that his compensation for losses sustained has increased and may even cover the whole financial loss caused by nonpayment.

ECA. The role of the insurer, who acts simultaneously as an Export Credit Agency, is even more important in debt collection and recoveries connected with insurance of political risks. The latter, for example, salvage or recovery measures may be better carried out by the ECA or its country government, either bilaterally or under the Paris Club negotiations. ECA status alone is a much weighty guarantee for success, because it may count on State support and assistance of their representatives. As a sovereign entity, the State is in a privileged position as a business partner or regulator of business activities, and likewise for the public company in relation to the private debtor. ECA is a substantially "more equal" party when it comes to negotiations and settlement of disputes. The role and mechanisms available to an ECA are even more important for the insured if the debtors are sovereign entities, public companies, or guarantors, or in the case of other political risks. Nowadays, this might be crucial, because in contemporary business, the formerly-clear boundaries between commercial and interlaced political risks are sometimes blurred.

For the conclusion, let us finish with the remark that the credit insurance is a specialist and labor-intensive class of insurance business where underwriting and procedures for debt collection, claims payments, and subsequent recoveries often stretch over longer period of time.

2.2.5 Credit Insurance Enhances External Financing

Commercial banks and other credit institutions play very important role in financing of business and facilitating trade, and big majority of world trade relies on bank credits and other financial instruments. Many companies have only limited sources of external financing for their business operations (funding gap), being unfortunately often the necessity for successful business operations and growth of the company. Considering the usefulness of credit insurance, one must repeatedly stress that the need for external financing would not be that large if companies have credit insurance policies that protected them from the risk of payment default of their buyers. On the other side of the coin, supplier credits can be important source of external finance to financially constrained companies because sellers involved in long-term relationships with their buyers might be better able to overcome enforcement problems and information asymmetry than financial institutions; especially during turmoil in the global financial markets characterized by severe credit crunch and with the credit insurance companies "on board."

The above is even truer for SMEs and other fast growing companies ("gazelles"), which record large growth rates and more or less have to rely on their own sources. However, these sources are often too small or at least inadequate. Nonperforming loans and payment defaults are driving reason for lenders to limit advances on pledged trade receivables and therefore limit the amount of working capital available. Moreover, it is usually more suitable for the companies to use external financing to achieve better business results. Due to the dominating position of the buyers on the market (buyers' markets), sellers are required to have financial sources and access to financing on favorable terms. This is the only way to take advantage of business opportunities on demanding markets and succeed against harsh competition.

Bank loans and credits and trade credits are often complements but can be substitutes as well. Supplier credits provide an alternative source of funds and allow eased external financing and higher growth in some industries and markets.

The lack of information and uncertainty as well as limited own sources and (in)availability of guarantees—the portfolio of insured accounts receivable is an excellent security for the bank acting as a lender and often the most favorable if not the only possible collateral available to the borrower as a security for loan repayment—as well as their price and other terms, restrict the options of companies for external financing of their business operations, production, and sales. Lenders, banks, and other financial institutions may have an otherwise negative attitude toward such companies and may decide not to lend them enough sources or grant them access to financial funds under strained conditions. For the banks and their business among various risks, the credit risk is usually the most important one. Banks are unwilling to extend loans to companies that do not meet the loan criteria and are not insured against risk of nonpayment. Prior to approval of the loan, they will check how the company is managing risks and how its trade receivables are insured. Banks observe, use, and handle credit insurance policies as a useful protective instrument that enables and increases the chances for financing their clients. Some of them will even insist on credit insurance before providing financing. On the other hand, risk premiums that are included in the borrowing costs mean that for the uninsured companies and their business operations higher interest rates, or a discount at invoice discounting, are charged; their interest rates may be so high that they endanger the competitiveness of the enterprises.

The acquisition of working capital, required for financing of business, **is made easier with credit insurance policies because they allow companies easier access to financial sources. Credit insurance improves the credit rating of a company**. Banks and other credit institutions, for example, factoring companies, are well aware that credit insurance policies cover important companies' assets—trade receivables. Such insurance gives them at least additional comfort, but could be financial security as well, meaning that the credit risk of financial institutions can be significantly reduced. On the other hand, **credit insurance gives companies the opportunity to increase their credit lines, hire loans, or sell their discounted trade receivables under more favorable terms**. Moreover, it enables them to preserve other remaining assets for other or future borrowing needs.

Trade finance is traditionally perceived as one of the safest, most collateralized and self-liquidating short-term lending. It can be also important that banks, according to regulation and their capital adequacy requirements for credit risks, might not need to build up special provisions for insured credits—for example, if the accounts receivable are insured with ECAs—or these provisions can be lower. As far as banks are concerned, provisions are regarded as costs. Therefore, credit insurance "improves the credit rating of bank customers" and credit insurance policy, especially if considered by banks and national regulators as collateral instrument eligible for recognition in implemented simple (standardized) approach under the Basel II capital accord (e.g., comprehensive insurance can sometimes even lead to zero-risk weighted), or even perhaps as a first-class security, can additionally reduce the costs of hiring loans for working capital. Anyway, credit insurance will be considered as a first-class security only in extremely exceptional cases, as credit insurance can be direct and explicit, but not also fully irrevocable and unconditional security.

Assignment of Insurance Policy Rights

To use credit insurance policy as a financial instrument to lay off credit risk and to obtain trade financing or to hire loans on more favorable terms and conditions is a common purpose for (collateral) assignment of insurance policy rights. Banks use such assignments even more frequently in other types of credit insurance, for example, for consumer credits, where life or fire insurance policies are required. But the solution with the seller/exporter as the insured assigning claim proceeds to financing bank as a loss payee is nevertheless quite frequently used in trade finance too.

Assignment of proceeds from an insurance contract may consist of two "unilateral contracts": with the first authorization the insured party authorizes the insurance company to pay the claim directly to the bank and with the second one it authorizes the bank to accept this payment.

With an assignment of the policy rights (see also in Section 4.2.1)—as a whole or for each business separately—of the insured (assignor) that arises from the insurance contract, whereas the bank (assignee) cannot acquire more rights than the insured and the insurance company (debtor) must agree with the assignment, the lending bank may get the claim paid upon the occurrence of the loss-causing event directly from the insurer and not through the insured party.

Because many countries require the insurance contracts to be in writing, it is even more generally accepted rule that the assignments or transfers of the credit insurance policy or any of its benefit is not valid without prior written consent of the insurer. General insurance conditions usually also provide that through the assignment of rights from the insurance contract, the insured remains the insured party and is not discharged or relieved from his liabilities toward the insurer, that is, disclosure and reporting duty and payment of insurance premium. Any objection, exclusion, set-off, or forfeiture otherwise addressed to the insured by the insurer can be used against the assignee as well, and the rights of the latter are not independent from the underlying insurance contract concluded between the insurer and the insured. The **request for claims payment** or the facts and circumstances regarding the occurrence of the loss-causing event will be normally handled only between the insurance company and the insured. The latter is, in principle, obliged to file the claim, while the proceeds from his rights arising out of the insurance contract are directly effected to the lending bank (assignee).

Claims payment provoked by bankruptcy or protracted default may not always be clear-cut and the insured's request may be declined for the reasons stemming from the insurance conditions, that is, failure of the insured company to comply with his obligations toward the insurer, disputed debts (performance risk of the seller is not covered under the credit insurance policy), uncovered risks, and nonpayment of insurance premiume. The banks need to be as much as possible confident that their clients manage credit insurance policy properly and not imperil insurance coverage through a breach of insurance conditions. They may also agree with the insured parties on arrangement to ensure exchange of information and that their obligations are not neglected. Considering all these, the credit insurance policy may be regarded as an additional comfort or as a conditional financial instrument, that is, "imperfect security," from the bank's viewpoint.

The underwriters in the private insurance sector are traditionally still reluctant to offer credit insurance cover directly to banks. But it is also possible in practice, especially in medium-term credit insurance, that the financing bank concludes its own insurance contract as the insured party. This may be preferable, as it avoids the risk of the (inexperienced) seller voiding the insurance contract by failing to comply with the insurance conditions.

Credit insurance is primarily an insurance instrument—instrument of protection against risk—and not a financing instrument or a source of liquidity in itself, even though it enhances the creditworthiness of the buyer and may enable or facilitate financing of business operations. However, it is still a financial instrument being issued by financial institutions—credit insurance companies and ECAs.

Domestic and international trade nowadays rely heavily on trade finance provided by banks and other financial institutions. There are strong evidences that shrinking trade finance contributes to the world trade decline. Credit insurance can help companies in their collaboration with financial institutions and other business partners; it facilitates their external financing and enables them to get better credit terms from banks and other credit institutions. *Inter alia* credit insurance improves **credit rating** of companies, gives them better credibility in the eyes of their business partners and, at the same time, improves their reliability and **creditworthiness**. It is important for **banks** and other financial institutions as well as, to the same extent, for their **suppliers** and other business partners, as insured companies may get **better sales and payment terms and conditions**, that is, sales on credit or deferred payment terms without additional securities that should otherwise be provided by the buyer for the supplied goods and services. In brief, credit insurance performs various useful functions complementary to those of banks and other institutions.

CHAPTER 3

Basics and Principles of Credit Insurance

3.1 MAIN FEATURES AND CREDIT INSURANCE TERMINOLOGY

3.1.1 Short-, Medium-, and Long-Term Credits

In contrast to the term **export finance**, used in international trade for financing of larger transactions, exports of goods and services, especially capital or quasi-capital goods, equipment, and civil works that require crediting exceeding the term of 1 year due to their nature, for the financing of exports of consumer goods, spare parts, raw materials, and semi-finished products, the expression **trade finance** is used in international trade, which usually designates **short-term crediting** (mostly credits and

Credit Insurance. DOI: http://dx.doi.org/10.1016/B978-0-12-411458-6.00003-4

loans with a tenor of 90 or 180 days and up to 1 year, exceptionally even 2 years) or sales on deferred payment terms. The bulk of international trade consists of such exports. According to estimation, as much as 90 percent of the world's trade is conducted on the basis of cash payment at delivery or on short-term credits.

Essentially, this book concentrates and deals with the latter, that is, short-term commercial credits or business-to-business (B2B) trade receivables, and not with medium- (mostly 1 and 2–5 years) and long-term credits from 5 to 10 years and more. It mostly deals with short-term credit insurance against commercial and other marketable risks, which may be ceded by the primary insurers to the global private reinsurance market.

3.1.2 Supplier and Buyer Credits

Supplier credits are commonly used for short-term crediting and are extended by suppliers (exporters) to their buyers (importers) while the refinancing may take place in the form of invoice discounting or by, for example, assignment of the proceeds arising from credit insurance policy rights. As illustrated in Figure 3.1, in this traditional and straightforward model, the seller contracts goods and/or services to the buyer and the credit terms are included in their commercial contract.

1. Exporter concludes the insurance contract with the credit insurance company and pays the insurance premium.
2. Exporter's bank (based on the assignment of the insurance policy rights—1a) grants the credit to exporter/purchase accounts receivable.
3. Exporter delivers goods to buyer on deferred payment terms.
4. Buyer or his commercial bank—guarantor (4a) effects payments of the amounts due.

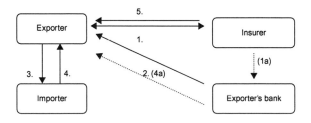

Figure 3.1 Supplier credit. See text for details.

5. If the buyer does not repay the credit, or the commercial bank acting as a guarantor does not pay, the credit insurer pays claim to the exporter (or to the exporter's bank on the basis of assignment of insurance policy rights—1a).

Buyer credits for the payments to suppliers are approved by the seller's or exporter's commercial bank to the buyers or their banks (on-lending to a client); sometimes this may be in the form of **general purpose** or **project line of credit**, either for export of variety of goods and/or services or for the needs of a particular large project. This main technique is usually used for medium- and long-term export credits. In addition to a commercial contract between the exporter and the importer, there is also a separate and parallel loan agreement concluded between their banks. The exporter is paid by its bank mainly on a cash basis by drawing of the loan after the commissioning or completion. The borrowing bank, backed by the agreement with the importer, then repays the loan to the lending bank, for example, in a preagreed loan period after the completion. Figure 3.2 illustrates the process and relations between the parties of the underlying commercial contract, banks involved in the transaction, and the credit insurer.

1. On the basis of credit contract with a foreign buyer (1a) or its bank (1b), the exporter's bank concludes an insurance contract (1c) with an ECA and pays insurance premium.
2. Buyer effects an advance payment to the exporter.
3. Exporter delivers goods according to the commercial contract and/or performs services.
4. Bank approves credit disbursements according to commercial contract, that is, it pays the exporter.

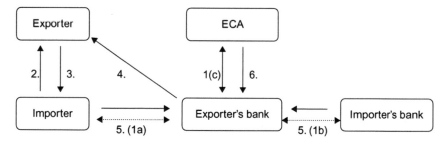

Figure 3.2 Buyer credit. See text for details.

5. Buyer or his commercial bank effects installment payments (principal and interest of the credit).
6. If buyer or his commercial bank (debtor or guarantor) does not pay the debt, ECA pays the claim to the exporter's bank.

3.1.3 General Insurance Principles

Although credit insurance has some special characteristics, such as long-term and labor-intensive cooperation between the partners and more active day-to-day involvement of the insured in policy management, it is nevertheless founded on the same **basic principles** as other property insurances as:

— the principle of mutuality and solidarity,
— the law of probability,
— the law of large numbers, and
— dispersion of risks underwritten by the insurer.

Credit insurance is usually an optimal way of ensuring that a loss incurred from any individual payment default is covered by spreading the risk over large population of insured companies (insurance premium payers) where relatively small premiums cover large potential losses.

These economic pillars and specifics are also important for proper understanding of credit insurance legal specifics in comparison with other institutes of law on obligations. Conclusion and implementation of credit insurance contract as a **contract of indemnity** mostly follows similar general legal principles as in other obligations, as well as other trust-based contracts and other types of property insurance, such as:

— the principle of autonomy or freedom of the contracting party to choose the counterparty, the type of contract, and its contents;
— *pacta sunt servanda*;
— the principle of good faith (*contractus bonae fidei* and fair dealing)—already known in Roman law—for the conclusion and implementation of contracts; for (credit) insurance (*Rozanes v. Bowen* (1928), 32 L.I.L.R. 98) even "utmost good faith" (*uberrimae fidei*) codified for marine insurance purposes is required (see, e.g., *Black King Shipping Corp. v. Massie, The Litsion Pride* (1985), 1 Lloyd's Rep. 437);
— insurable interest;

- principle of indemnity, that is, insurer's liability is restricted to the actual loss suffered and subject to the insurance contract limits and conditions;
- prohibition of unjust enrichment;
- "all-or-nothing" rule (however, only liability insurance allows the connection of legal contentiousness and liability for damage with the amount of the claims paid), etc.

If the credit insurance should be economically successful, the covered loss-causing events must be relatively independent. Supposing the past experiences are good bases for prediction of future results, the credit insurer must dispose of sufficient insurance capacities, know-how and risk management skills, as well as experience with this business field and track record.

3.1.4 Whole Turnover Insurance and Insurance of Individual (Specific) Transactions

ELIGIBLE TRANSACTIONS. The subject matter of credit insurance is the policyholder's financial interest in granted short-term commercial credits. Short-term credits are usually given in domestic and international trade for raw materials, consumer durables, spare parts, and semifinished goods, while machinery, equipment, and other capital or quasi-capital goods as well as civil works require longer credit periods. Almost all business transactions are eligible for the insurance of supplier's short-term credits—all legal trade with tradable goods and/or services. However, some business transactions may not be eligible for credit insurance due to different reasons arising from the traded goods and services (e.g., export of weapons and ammunition, radioactive and some psychotropic substances, prostitution—as a rule the latter used to be mostly based on cash payments). The insurance cover for trade receivables arising from specific business operations, for example, leasing contracts, may require special insurance conditions due to the characteristics of such business deals.

At first sight, it may seem there is no big difference between **commercial** and pure **financial credits** regarding the risks and credit rating of debtors, but the sole fact that commercial credits facilitate the flows of goods, gives the insurer in principle more comfort or certainty that the supplier credit will be repaid.

When granting **insurance for short-term credits against commercial risks**, the credit insurer tends to achieve good spread of risks in order to protect itself from the **concentration of risk** to particular buyers, industries, and countries as well as against the **adverse selection** of the insured who prefers to insure problematic buyers only and save insurance premium by leaving "solid" buyers uninsured. Therefore, an **insurance company would insist, at least in principle, to take over the entire portfolio of risks (all buyers) of the insured**, approving their insurance (credit) limits—in case of smaller turnover with a particular buyer, an "automatic" insurance limit will be set without special credit checking—meaning that in practice, this insurance will be close to **whole turnover insurance policies**. Even though the credit insurers underwrite most of the individual risks, usually every effort is made to avoid adverse selection as much as possible. However, in practice credit insurance companies would allow certain justified selection of buyers, especially when large companies and volume of their business insured are in question. But nevertheless in their underwriting and marketing, they would stand by the principle of well-dispersed portfolio, that is, **spread cover**, giving underwriters a sufficient spread of risk and adequate insurance premium.

Especially with SMEs whose limited trade volume and poor sales dispersion prevents the selection of buyers, an insurer will, in principle, stick to **whole turnover insurance policies**, that is, the insurance of all (insurable) short-term trade receivables against foreign and/or domestic buyers, which are included in insurance by being granted an insurance limit. There are also exceptions for buyers coming from particular countries, regions, or industries as well as regarding types of goods, payment terms, or even regarding individual buyers. Sometimes, at the beginning of business cooperation between exporter and credit insurer, the insurance cover may be relatively narrow and consequently new buyers are added with annexes to the original insurance contract.

Certainly, the insurance of the whole credit sales of the insured who transfers an adequately dispersed risk portfolio to the insurer may result in much lower insurance premium rates than the premium rates for specific transaction or transactions, including successive deliveries, with the selected buyer, that is, **single buyer insurance policy**.

Adverse Selection and Moral Hazard

There are several market failures and the insurance market is not immune to them, meaning there is always the possibility of inefficient resource allocation or that the market cannot work at all. The **asymmetric**

information is still, but may be less important for credit insurance as for other insurance classes and it comes in two forms: **adverse selection** and **moral hazard**.

1. Regarding the first problem of credit insurance linked is the imperfection of information—adverse selection, information asymmetry exists before the insurance contract is concluded, especially in commercial risk insurance, if the insured is aware of certain characteristics (hidden information) that could have a material impact on the profitability of the business relationship and cannot be fully known by the insurer; which means the insurer is not in a position to consider them in underwriting and establishing appropriate insurance premium rate. Otherwise, it is a general rule that companies who decide for credit insurance are more exposed to risk of nonpayment of their buyers or are at least more aware of the fact and cannot afford payment defaults.

2. On the other hand, moral hazard may cause the policyholder to take more and larger risks as he would be without insurance and to enter into business with less caution and with less effort to prevent loss-causing events and minimize their consequences. In brief, moral hazard means a negative effect on incentives for self-protection by the insured party.

Even though commercial and noncommercial credit risks are mostly exogenous, the moral hazard in credit insurance consists mainly of asymmetry of information after the insurance contract is concluded—even in cases when the insured could react in some way to prevent or minimize the loss, but the insurer is not in a position to detect and know it in detail. Therefore, these measures cannot be a part of the insurance contract. If these measures were too hard for the insured, they may stimulate him toward suboptimal activities for preventing or minimizing losses (here we mean hidden actions or behavior of the insured).

Insurers fight against these market failures (Pareto inefficiency) with specially created offers of credit insurances and characteristics of their instruments. They fight against the adverse selection of risks, especially of commercial risks, mainly with the **request that the whole turnover of the insured must be offered for insurance and by nonlinear pricing**.

Another preventive measure may also be the *bonus* system of insurance premium, for example, no claim bonus (sometimes in credit insurance also *malus* or combination of *bonus* and *malus*), in which the insured has the right to partial repayment of insurance premium if the loss recorded in the previous period (e.g., in the last 3 years) was favorable and the insured states that he has no claims against his debtors ("profit sharing"). But it is seldom in practice that the insured is entitled to a reduced insurance premium rates in the next accounting insurance period.

On the other hand, the moral hazard is fought mostly:

1. with the selection and checking of the partner (the insured party);
2. by refusing to insure credits to affiliated persons;
3. by demanding that the insured behaves as if he is uninsured when doing business with his buyers;
4. by using the **"conditionality"** of the instrument of credit insurance—if the insured does not fulfill his obligations from the insurance contract, he is threatened by sanctions, for example, rejection of claims payments or reduced claims paid, cancellation of insurance contract; and
5. with **self-retention** of the insured.

Such deductible mainly depends on the type of the risk insured and the quality of the company's trade receivable accounts. It is required and set such that the insured party still has an incentive to manage its risks and trade relations. In short-term credit insurance against commercial risks, the insured's self-retention usually amounts to 10 or 15 percent. On the other hand, in case of noncommercial risks beyond the control and influence of the insured it can be even smaller, meaning that the percentage of insurance cover against political and other noncommercial risks may be even higher, even 100 percent.

3.1.5 Main Features of Credit Insurance Cover

SPREAD OF RISK. Standard credit insurance policies—with variations across the market—for the trade on domestic and/or foreign markets are founded on more or less strict templates and traditional or "old-fashioned" principles of **whole turnover insurance** (global insurance policies). This is rather logical requirement and attitude since the insurers need to disperse risks underwritten and try to avoid adverse selection but cannot always be achieved. The above principle is therefore often replaced by "more realistic" and also acceptable **spread insurance cover**, which is, at least to a certain extent, always considered in credit insurance where:

— the insurance is granted within the framework of a **general contract on credit insurance** (revolving system), while on the other hand,
— insurance for individual transactions may sometimes be granted by **specific (account) insurance policies**, which cover certain risks on facultative bases, for example, specific account policies, country

turnover policies, single account policies, or policies for insurance of payment default risks arising from a particular commercial contract.

CREDIT INSURANCE POLICIES. The structure of a particular credit insurance policy can be quite flexible in response to competition and might be tailor-made to reflect particular features of the insured's trade and the volume of its business insured. Along with prevailing whole turnover insurance policy and its variants—**multiple market policy** and **country turnover policy**—there are also other options available to companies with large and dispersed trade pattern, that is, **nonproportional insurance cover**, sometimes also called catastrophe coverage, for agreed selection of risks. Such nonproportional insurance cover provides the insured an economic security above a certain level, and in principle, this coverage is cheaper than a whole turnover insurance policy. Up to this level, a company is able to retain the risks by itself and can use sophisticated techniques and methods of risk management. Some credit insurers offer insurance coverage that protects only some sections of companies' operations, for example, the risk of a **key buyer (principal customer/specific/top account cover)**, which may significantly influence the companies' balance sheets, while the insured alone deals with the risks of minor buyers or low-value orders. Due to poor dispersion of risks and demanding management of the insurance policy, such insurance is more expensive for policyholders than whole turnover insurance.

- **PROPORTIONAL INSURANCE.** In fact, whole turnover insurance is usually **proportional insurance coverage**, where the insurer assumes the agreed share for every risk insured (unpaid invoice amount) above the self-retention of the insured—insurance against commercial risk usually has such "deductible" of 15 percent—which is similar to **surplus insurance**.

- **NONPROPORTIONAL INSURANCE.** Another option—above all for larger companies with the substantial business insured and who prefer cover against large losses only, which may threaten their solvency and would like to keep the larger part of their insurance premium as well as to reduce the costs of administrative procedures—is **nonproportional insurance**, for example, **excess of loss** or **stop loss insurance**. By the former, with the stipulation of **exclusion clauses**, the (re)insurer takes over the risks above the uninsured retention up to a maximum amount agreed upon, or even up to the total **sum insured**, but not fully for each and every claim. Such nonproportional insurance cover, sometimes also referred to catastrophe insurance, provides a layer of protection for losses sustained beyond a certain affordable level with significant impact on the balance sheet of the company. It is appropriate for those who want to be insured against single larger losses and are more interested in balance sheet than cash-flow protection. On the other hand, stop loss insurance is used when the company would like to limit the effects of accumulation of losses, when the insurer does not cover the risk for each or every claim but only for particularly severe or catastrophic claims above a certain loss ratio. For **threshold insurance cover**, the insurance contract provides that claims under a certain limit (nonqualifying losses) that are borne by the insured and are not covered by the insurer. However, once the threshold level is exceeded, the insurer will pay the total value of claim reduced by the insured's self-retention. Some insurance contracts may even cap the aggregate maximum claims paid in a certain policy period, for example, 1 year. This aggregate—**insurer's maximum liability (IML)** − is defined on the basis of the largest approved insurance limit or on a multiple of annual insurance premium paid. It is worth mentioning that the IML should be sufficient to cover catastrophic loss, for example, political risk that may disrupt wider region, but that would certainly have an impact on the premium rates.

As a rule, **the subject matters of credit insurance are short-term trade receivables** denominated **in monetary terms** (*in valora*). The latter—monetary/pecuniary obligations—also far prevail in modern business practice of all civilized money- and credit-based economies.

COUNTERTRADE. Due to specific problems, accounts receivable (*in natura*) from various types of **countertrade**, for example, counter-purchase or barter deals, may be insured only exceptionally and under special conditions. But even insured countertrade receivables normally must be expressed in hard (convertible) currency, while the goods of the buyer, that is, the "means of payment" for the seller's goods or services, must be of standard quality and the "price" and quantity must be clearly defined in the commercial contract. There must also be a "liquid" market available for the goods ("marketability of the goods"), being a subject matter of counter-deliveries.

If not otherwise provided by the insurance contract, only the principal (*sortem*) of the credit is covered by the credit insurance, while regular contractual interest (*usuras*) and/or default interest, penalties (*poenae conventionalis*), and other means intended to strengthen the obligations of the buyer are usually not covered. Otherwise, regular interest is hardly ever seen in sales on deferred payment terms or short-term credits.

VALID UNDERLYING TRANSACTION. A condition precedent for validity and effectiveness of insurance coverage is that the credit sale subject matter, that is, delivered goods and/or performed services, must be part of a legally valid transaction and that commercial agreement between the buyer and the insured is not in contradiction with applicable mandatory laws (*contra legem*).

CURRENCY. The insured accounts receivable may be denominated and payable in **domestic currency** (as a rule in the insurance of domestic credits). If not in contradiction with mandatory provisions of the monetary and/or foreign exchange regulations, the insured accounts receivable may be—according to the insurance conditions and business policy of the insurer, especially in export credit insurance—denominated, for either one or both insurance contract parties, in freely transferable **foreign currency** or composite currency unit, where the foreign currency may only be the currency of the account or payment, respectively.

The short-term credit insurance is merely **the insurance of accounts receivable arising from sales on deferred payment terms**. The characteristics of downpayments and cash or spot payments are that in the latter case contracting parties fulfill their obligations at the same time. Therefore, there is no credit involved and, consequently, there is also no repayment risk, which means the company does not need to insure such sales, but nevertheless, the insured must report such advance payments to the insurer anyway.

— As a rule, the insured is not obliged to insure **contracts with associated persons** (intragroup trade). If the insured sells goods to an associated company, this is especially true for "downstream" sales to a daughter company, which is under the control of the insured and the insured may influence his business with the subsidiary. In other words, the insured is thus in a position to influence the occurrence of the insured event. In such a case, the credit insurer most probably would not be willing to cover such business transactions, or at least would not insure it against commercial risks, which are almost nonexistent in such transactions. On the other hand, trade between affiliated persons might be insured against political risks, for example, risk on despatched merchandize in transport caused by political incidents. If credits between affiliated persons were insured, the insured might fall to temptation and act "opportunistically" by trying to gain unjust enrichment, for example, through insurance fraud. Undeniably, there is always some moral hazard involved—which insurers try to avoid—in the insurance of credits extended to daughter companies due to specifics of these assets and "information asymmetry," which is in favor of the insured. To avoid such moral hazard, the insurer will normally refuse to insure the risk of trade between associated persons and will only agree to cover it exceptionally, under special conditions or limited to political risk coverage.

— Moreover, the insured normally does not need to insure credits where he as a seller has already agreed on certain securities, for example, irrevocable, unconditional, and independent **bank guarantee** or **L/C** issued or confirmed by the first-class bank from a low-risk country. Certainly, the credit insurance policy may efficiently replace such securities provided by the buyer to cover his liabilities. Above all, long-term transactions or business deals with the buyers in high-risk countries may require such securities, perhaps also as a precondition for the issuance of the credit insurance policy.

— Sometimes the insured also does not need to insure his sales transacted and invoiced for payment cash against documents **(CAD)**. However, these transactions are also insured but under special conditions. In such a case, sales on CAD terms are considered as sales made on terms leaving the insured with the control of the goods until full payment is made to the person instructed to present the documents; insurance policy covers arbitrary refusal of the buyer to accept goods due to his insolvency and the insured is compensated for resale of returned merchandize.

CREDIT AND MANUFACTURING RISK. Regarding the characteristics of the sales of the insured party, it is certainly possible that **preshipment manufacturing risks insurance**, as supplementary insurance coverage for the **postshipment credit risk insurance**, covers only part of the total sales of a particular exporter; meaning that preshipment risk insurance cover against cancellation or contract revoking, if underwritten by the insurer, would be approved also for private buyers, for a particular sales contract or its part, as well as for specific sales to individual buyer.

The "automatic" insurance limits mentioned before are applied for smaller amounts. To save time and simplify administrative procedures for buyers with negligible debts, they can be excluded from the insurance contract. In practice, we come upon insurance policies that cover only key customers, nonproportional insurances, etc.

3.1.6 Prices of Insurance Services

It is often difficult to determine the price of an intangible goods and services, whose values may differ for one or another customer. Pricing should reflect also the influence of competition and substitutes. Even insurance companies have problems with pricing and the "trial-and-error" method may have an unfavorable impact on their business results. When the risks of nonpayments are transferred to a credit insurance company, they are transformed into underwriting/insurance risks, so the insurance premiums are not sufficient to cover the claims paid and insurance operating costs.

Based on the laws of probability and large numbers, credit insurance also works on a funding principle to pool collected insurance premiums from the insured parties to form a fund for paying the claims of some of them who suffer losses. Besides fixing the prices of their insurance products, before they are aware of all possible costs and implementing actuarial analysis and models, insurers must also consider claims and loss ratios as the main determinant of their supply, their risk portfolio, as well as some fundamental assumptions, that is, normal pattern of losses and the facts that they underwrite numerous and homogeneous units of their risk portfolio, which are exposed to loss-causing events statistically independent and, most importantly, whether their past experiences are good enough basis to predict future, as well as to properly anticipate changes of factors influencing the risks underwritten and loss-causing events when they calculate the price of their services (premium rates). They must be also able to correctly anticipate the changing risk, build reserves, and adjust their premium rates to follow the frequency and severity of the risk underwritten as well as the volatility of the insurer's business result. On the other hand, competition and other factors impose constraint on the size of provisions and contingency loading to premium rates.

If we leave out reinsurance and the need to generate sufficient income, including investment earnings for employed capital, the insurer must therefore collect insurance premiums that would at least cover all risks underwritten. Considering the cash flow, they represent the net present value (NPV) of the insurer's loss expectancy and other future liabilities according to the following simplified equation:

$$P = [(q \times l) + c + o + p] - I$$

where

P = insurance premium;
q = probability of loss-causing event;
l = average size of loss that occurs;
c = costs of provisioning;
o = operating costs (acquiring new clients, insurance policies management, prevention, claims handling, debt collection, recoveries, etc.);
p = target profit;
I = investment earnings.

Unfortunately, this does not say much about actual credit insurance pricing. The price of insurance or the premium rate is indeed a very important essential element of an insurance contract and, at the same time, it is a calculative element and cost considered by the companies when they enter into an insurance contract on the basis of their risk perception and the need for economic security.

As a matter of fact, credit insurance services are not easy to sell for the price that reflects the portfolio of the risks underwritten. Insurance is an "invisible" service or conditional "promise" of an insurance company to pay claim in case of occurrence of uncertain and future loss-causing event. The demand for credit insurance has low-price elasticity that applies only for high-risk insurance business. The insured pays insurance premium up-front, while the obligation of the insurer is conditional upon the occurrence of the insured event, which is a future and uncertain in time when an insurance contract is concluded. Therefore, the insured often speculates with the possibility that the damage will not occur. As credit insurance is about the promise of the insurance company, the insured has practically no way of estimating the reliability and quality of offered services, except at the stage of claims handling (*ex post*). Yet promised or guaranteed economic safety does not come for free, even though the loss-causing event never occurs.

Like all prices, credit insurance premium rates also depend on supply and demand, which are functions of numerous factors. An acceptable price for the insured is one for which the marginal benefit of protection against risks or added value of the insurance services is larger than the benefit of "lost" additional units of income.

Economic crises definitely have great influence on these factors. But on the other hand, reinsurance markets play a very important role too. It is well known that reinsurance undergoes alternating periods of soft and hard markets, where in the latter case premium rates are growing and capacities and coverage supply are restricted.

The insurance premium *inter alia* depends on spread of risk offered to insurer as well as on percentage of insurance cover. The insurance premium for whole turnover policy is therefore significantly lower than the insurance of an individual transaction.

Even though the credit insurers assess the credit rating and particular risk as well as underwrite the risks of the buyers individually, the decision on the insurance contract and conditions of insurance cover depends heavily on market and negotiating positions. Despite the fact that credit insurers are rather flexible, the decisions will be based on the size and quality of the portfolio and dispersion of risks underwritten. Therefore, it may happen that the insurer will not issue the policy to particular company although it offers to insure its whole turnover, because the risk portfolio may not be good enough or insufficiently dispersed. Risk equalization is economically not possible without establishing a suitable homogeneous risk group. To be able to form the above group (the "consolidation of risks"), sufficient and adequately dispersed multitude is required, because only then the laws of probability and large numbers could take effect.

ADVERSE SELECTION. The insured must therefore abandon the selection of good risks only. This follows from one of the basic insurance principles, that is, the underwriters always consider the volume and risk dispersion or mutuality as well as risk totality to prevent adverse selection of the insured. The other basic principle of credit insurance is that the insurer is a partner of the insured who follows the fortune of his business operations and the loss results. The partnership should be long-term oriented, meaning it is not limited to good times only. Experience taught us that the adverse selection of risks is often not worthwhile for the company entering into an insurance contract and the question is whether the insurer is willing to conclude such a contract at all.

Even solid buyers may get worse or even go bankrupt. They may be stricken by various unforeseen circumstances or get into troubles because of nonpayment of their customers. Numerous bankruptcies are caused by the insolvency of key customers.

Circumstances that make credit risk management difficult also include debtor's status changes, alterations of ownership structure, privatization as well as establishment of new enterprises. It is quite common in insurance practice to meet entrepreneurs who, after many years of successful cooperation with the reputable partner, walk away empty-handed despite knowing their customers well.

Personal acquaintance may promote sales but does not help much when companies are not financially sound or capable of repaying their debts.

The price paid for economic security by the insured—the insurance premium—reflects each adverse selection or quality of the risk portfolio offered to the underwriter. Time after time it pays the insured to insure all of its accounts receivable toward all of its buyers.

Sometimes, on the basis of anticipated and actual volume of business insured to obtain envisaged premium income of the insurer, the insurance contract may prescribe a **minimum annual premium** and premium rates increase depending on the discrepancy between the actual and the anticipated sales turnover.

Insurance Premium Rates

According to the equivalence principle, credit insurance premium rates reflect firstly the risk portfolio quality and dispersion of underwritten risks.

Insurance premium always reflects the capability and readiness of the insurer to take over certain risks considering the existing and potential competition, reinsurance capacities, its underwriting results and costs of capital employed, etc. Credit insurance premium rates are in practice is usually determined on the basis of the factors stated below:

- expected volume of business insured;
- weighted—by the business insured/insurance limits—average payment terms, eventually increased by average payment delays (longer term—greater risk);
- percentage of insurance cover;
- number of buyers, credit amounts, and dispersion of sales or spread of risk among countries, industries, and buyers;

- debtor's credit ratings;
- buyer's branches;
- country risks;
- previous loss and other experiences of the insured as well as payment discipline of his buyers;
- credit risk management and securities in use (e.g., ROT), etc.

Specialization of credit insurers and harsh competition in the credit insurance market as well as existence of various other instruments of protection against payment default risks—sometimes they are more or less perfect substitutes—always put credit insurance premiums within reasonable and relatively low level and provide assurance of appropriate compensation for business safety created by insurance company.

Insurances offered by officially supported **ECAs** are mostly oriented to one-off business operations or insurance of individual medium-term export credits. Their tariffs differ from one agency to another but are based on similar principles. The prices—at least the premium rates for medium-term export credit insurance against the most important political risks (country and sovereign credit risk)—are globally more or less harmonized. ECAs from developed national economies strive to operate transparently, to enforce international discipline in this field and want to avoid credit wars that would stimulate exports with too low premium rates and other favorable financing and insurance terms and conditions rather than prices, quality of the products, and other competitive advantages.

As a rule, ECAs collect insurance premiums up-front, that is, after conclusion of insurance contract but payment in installments aligned with the disbursement of the loans can also be arranged. Insurance premiums of national ECAs are risk based and depend on a number of variables, for example:

- classification of buyer's/debtor's or guarantor's country in one of the risk categories (typically seven or eight);
- public or private status of debtor or guarantor;
- buyer's or guarantor's credit rating;
- percentage of cover (PC);
- length of credit or horizon of risk (HOR); and
- security package available (escrow accounts, bank guarantees, and similar undertakings).

CALCULATION OF INSURANCE PREMIUM. Credit insurance companies collect premiums on the basis of actual (reported) turnover, that is, **turnover declaring**. This is a simple and fair basis for insuring regular and successive deliveries. Another way of calculating insurance premiums in practice is more "exact"—at least in cases in which buyers have prolonged deferred payment terms—if the basis for calculation is **balance declaring** (outstanding debts), or premiums may be calculated according to insurance limits. The insurer must be regularly informed by the insured—usually on a monthly basis for the previous month—on all outstanding (new) debts of its buyers/debtors and insurance premiums paid depending on the actual trade volume.

Regular **reporting of all** insured **credits** including the ones already settled partly or in full, for example, discount for anticipated payment (*sconto cassa*), is an **essential contractual obligation of the insured** and a precondition of insurance coverage existence and validity as well as a basis for claims payment in case of a loss-causing event occurrence. **Underdeclaration** may have dire consequences on the insured, since his unreported accounts receivable are therefore not covered, and furthermore, other claims may also be proportionally reduced in such a case ("rule of proportion"). Moreover, the insurer is also entitled to terminate the insurance contract, if the insured does not fulfill his contractual obligations.

Insurance of Small- and Medium-Sized Enterprises

Small enterprises typically facing shortage of finance may also be handicapped by the nonpayment risk and may even be more endangered, as their other assets are not sufficient to overcome difficulties caused by payment defaults of their buyers. On the other hand, buyers can more easily afford themselves not to settle their due debts to such suppliers. Several SMEs are forced to cease their business operation due to bankruptcies or payment delays. Due to their limited potential for insurers, credit risk exposure to key customers and diseconomies of scale as well as high overheads, this niche market segment is often not very attractive for the insurance companies. Moreover, small companies typically lack trade experience and expertise in credit insurance as well as may need more assistance and advice in such rather difficult and technical matters. But if the insurers want to keep their reputation, they cannot afford to ignore SMEs.

Prices of all credit insurance services are often included in the **insurance premium**. Along with risks underwritten, they also contain other costs of the insurers such as administration of insurance policies, and so on. Insured parties with a smaller volume of business insured and many small invoices are cost-intensive and therefore less attractive for insurance companies. Credit insurers try to solve these problems with intensive transition to e-commerce, automatic insurance limits, and simplified claims handling in case of minor buyers (insurance limits) or small invoice amounts.

Credit insurers linked to the government (ECAs), especially, adapt their offer to the requirements of SMEs and even produce special facilities for this category of companies. Wording of their insurance policies and general insurance conditions is simplified and written in plain language, while the application for cover, policy administration, insurance declarations and reporting, premium collection, and claims handling are streamlined to ease the administrative burden to a minimum. Their credit insurance facilities for SMEs, that is, pure cover, can be combined with other financing facilities and products and may include their commercial banks as insurance policy managers, etc.

TAXATION AND ADDITIONAL FEES. Sometimes "undesired" insurance premium tax or other taxes and duties must be added to insurance premium to enable the state to perform its tasks as well as various **fees** and charges for credit information, processing of insurance limits and risk monitoring, costs for legal consultancy, debt collection, and judicial and other proceedings. The costs of these auxiliary services (serviced credit insurance) are usually charged separately, along with the insurance premium.

Due to harsh competition in the international financial markets and the effect of the law of large numbers as well as the advantages of this instrument of protection over other securities, the **prices of credit insurance** are **relatively low** and usually affordable, especially in comparison to risk exposure. Credit insurance enables companies to increase sales and gives them adequate protection against risks as well as brings them other benefits.

Compared to other insurance classes, credit insurance may not come cheap, but there are several reasons that justify the price. Firstly, credit insurance policies have powerful elements of risk management and therefore credit insurers do not sell financial protection only but credit risk management as well. As it is a labor-intensive activity, the work of the credit insurer does not end with the risk assessment and conclusion of an insurance contract. Secondly, credit insurance is also more capital-intensive than other insurance classes and financial protection provided by the credit insurance is exposed to cycles and involves large and possibly also catastrophic risks that may affect large amounts at once and strain (re)insurers' capacities. It is often said that insurance is as much an art as a science when it comes to catastrophe risk. And last but not least, credit insurance is a demanding and troubled type of insurance, for example, insurance premiums for this insurance class *inter alia* serve to form necessary provisions and equalization reserves to cover future losses and the risk equalization in credit insurance takes rather long period of time. Credit insurance is definitely among those insurance classes that are highly vulnerable to volatility because of exposure to economic cycles. Therefore, inherent imbalance must be spread over many years and contingency loadings need to be built into charged insurance premiums.

On the other hand, credit insurance premiums are much more than compensation for the damage caused by buyers' payment defaults, which is nevertheless main and the far most important function of a credit insurance. Insurance premium paid is a "guarantee" and compensation for provided economic security. From the viewpoint of the insured parties, it is therefore wrong to look at the credit insurance premium within the framework of their technical result. Nevertheless, it will not necessarily be the best predictor of their future business. The claims paid by the insurance company are *ex ante* certainly not the result wished by the insured at the time the insurance contract is concluded. The goal of the insured is just the opposite—to avoid the losses. In particular cases, that is, long-term cooperation with the insured and zero claims paid in the period of several years, credit insurers may consider giving such insured party **bonus** or reduced premium rates, while on the other hand, the insurance companies may also increase premium rates.

Bonus (*malus*)

Credit insurance and its pricing are, to a certain extent, subject to **individualization of premium rates** or **bonus system**. The *bonus* system—discount or price stimulation of the insured—is nevertheless far more frequent in other insurance classes, for example, other property insurances, where insurance premium depends on claims paid or not paid, for example, during previous 3 years period of time (no claim bonus), or on the number of insured events occurred in the previous period (loss record). Due to the nature of the insured risks, credit insurance is more or less limited in the process of "insurance premium individualization", because claims often occur randomly, while the equalization is a long-term process. *Malus* ("premium rate increase") is even rarer in credit insurance as the *bonus*. However, the insured and credit insurer may sometimes make an agreement providing that the insured will participate somehow in case of a favorable (or unfavorable) loss ratio. *Bonus* or *malus* can therefore be defined as percentage or amount of invoiced/paid insurance premium, which is returned to the insured party having predefined "good" loss record within the period of time defined in the insurance contract or has to be paid in addition in case of bad claims ratio. It is also possible that the loss record is taken into account in the next insurance period.

In spite of favorable claims experience, that is, none or very little claims paid, there is no assurance that the insurance premium rate will be reduced. On the contrary, insurance premium rates may even rise if the riskiness magnifies or the conditions in reinsurance market are aggravated (so called "hard market"). The insurance premium rates do not reflect the "history" or the insurance result, but the riskiness of the insured risk portfolio and are the result of supply and demand, which are functions of numerous other factors.

3.1.7 Pre- and Postshipment Risks

In sales on deferred payment terms despatched or delivered goods are usually beyond the physical control of the seller who may then only wait for his invoices to be paid at their maturity. In such a case, open account deliveries expose the seller to the **postshipment credit risk** of his buyer. This "principal" risk is real, since in the meantime the debtor may face liquidity problems and even become insolvent. On the other hand, some other events may occur in the credit period after the shipment or acceptance of goods as well, for example, discovered defects and dropping of market prices for merchandize, appreciation of the currency of the contract, which can lead to repudiation or can affect the buyer's willingness and capability to pay for goods under the original contract terms and conditions.

Moreover, in several lines of business ancillary and in various commercial transactions the seller can be exposed also to **preshipment manufacturing or financial risk** of the buyer and his host country. Loss-causing events, for example, bankruptcy, contract frustration and political risks of embargo, and cancellation or nonrenewal of import license, may happen either after or before the services are performed and the goods are actually shipped—in the latter case, when the goods are still in the production and under the disposition or surveillance of the seller. Due to the buyer's refusal to accept the goods and/or shipping documents, his repudiation and similar perils, also in the manufacturing or precredit period—after the conclusion or effectiveness of the underlying commercial contract being frustrated and before the goods are despatched or invoiced—the seller may thus bear various additional costs and work-in-progress losses, for example, expenses for raw materials, manufacturing costs, warehousing, and insurance costs. This precredit risk (PCR) is particularly important for sellers of goods they make to order, especially big and specific orders, suppliers of capital goods, equipment and other specially designed (custom-made) goods of high value with longer manufacturing period that cannot be resold or can be resold to another customer, but not in a desired time-frame or at original price. In such a case the seller will most probably suffer a loss in attempting to sell (distressed) goods elsewhere or in recovering materials for reuse. On the other hand, certain commercial transactions and some goods are due to their nature neither suitable nor eligible for preshipment risk cover, that is, perishable goods, transactions with the delivery date as a key factor, services charged on a man/day basis, etc.

PCR COVER. These preshipment or precompletion risks can be for prudent trader efficaciously covered with the credit insurance policy recompensation for work-in-progress on a commercial contract that is not capable of being fulfilled, thereby ensuring the insured reimbursement of net costs in case of occurrence of the insured event in the PCR (preshipment or precommissioning) period, that is, up to the time the credit period and ordinary postshipment credit insurance cover begins—traditionally 6–12 months between the effective date of contract and the (forecasted) date of each despatch of goods (or their acceptance) which is presumably when the seller invoice his buyer. This insurance cover varies in practice, but is usually designed to indemnify the insured for the costs of design, manufacturing, and supply of the goods which cannot be delivered, less any payments received and proceeds of their resale (realization value). PCR insurance normally does not cover liquidated damages and never provides claims payment in excess of the amounts received in case the contract had been fully executed (the limit is agreed insurance cover percentage of selling price of goods that are not delivered) and is traditionally limited to actual costs incurred, excluding fixed overheads or profits. However, some credit insurers allow claiming for an element of lost profit, while others may be willing to cover the proportion of overheads.

Most credit insurers do offer insurance cover also for preshipment risk, not so often and not on a stand-alone basis, but through a separate insurance policy or as its addition, rather than as part of their standard policy forms, that is, combined insurance policy. Of course, it is often possible that for each particular underlying commercial contract the pre- and postshipment insurance covers are in operation simultaneously in respect of different goods, some being manufactured while some are already shipped. In practice, preshipment cover provides protection for nonstandard goods which are by expectation difficult to resell, normally against the risk of insolvency of a private buyer, including perhaps political risk cover, while the debts of public buyers are insured also against the repudiation risk.

3.2 BASIC PRINCIPLES AND CREDIT INSURANCE CONDITIONS

Credit insurance policy provides the exporter or seller (creditor) who properly fulfills his contractual obligations efficient protection and according to applicable insurance conditions covers buyer's (debtor's) payment default risk in case of occurrence of the insured event by agreed claim payment.

Credit insurance conditions stipulate insurance coverage for **nonpayment** risk of the debtors caused by their **insolvency** (bankruptcies and similar events) and, if covered, **protracted default**, that is, nonpayment or delay in payment (*mora debitoris*)—typically, the insurance policy will specify a period between 90 and 180 days after the original due date but may be longer, for example, 9 or 12 months, for the markets with the customary prolonged late payments and longer time required for debt collection. Moreover, in addition to mentioned commercial and **political or noncommercial risk** comprehensive insurance coverage, since these risks may also lead to nonpayment, credit insurance conditions may cover **repudiation** risk and other fundamental **breach of contract** as well, particularly if public buyers are insured.

3.2.1 Insured Events—Definitions in Insurance Conditions
INSURANCE CONDITIONS AND RISKS COVERED. As any other insurance, credit insurance covers losses directly arising from the named

insured events, for example, bankruptcy, embargo, and similar loss-causing events or perils. There are different methods applied in general and/or special insurance conditions for defining which risks are insured. Insurance conditions *ex ante* stipulate general definitions of these events in more or less descriptive terms, which have to be tested for each particular case, especially *ex post* after the occurrence of the insured event in the claims handling procedures. Because circumstances of particular commercial transactions are not always clear-cut, and there are limitations of written language presented as well, this is not always an easy job and contracting parties may not share the same view about the crucial fact whether the particular risk is covered or not, or whether the circumstances of a loss-causing event fall within the defined insured event and which one. Nevertheless, by all means insurance conditions must be read carefully to be sure of the extent of the cover provided. In case of ambiguity, negotiations between the insurance contract parties, market customs, and case laws can play important role. The insured party is therefore, in principle, keen on obtaining comprehensive (*all risk*) credit insurance coverage for broad spectrum of possible loss-causing events, while on the other hand, the insurer would try to insist to limit his liabilities only to the named and described events and circumstances enabling him to assess the risks underwritten precisely as much as possible. In practice and in insurance conditions, in addition to general *positive* definition of the risks insured, these general definitions are complemented with the descriptive list of the named and described insured events and their circumstances (enumerative method), as well as with special usual or optional **exclusions** (*negative definitions*) and limitations of the insurer's liability. Of course, in case that certain risk is excluded, the onus of proof that the event occurred falls within named exclusion and that the loss was incurred because of such noninsured event as direct or indirect cause of loss rests with the insurer (*Spinneys (1948) Ltd. and Ors. v. Royal Insurance Co. (1980) Q.B. November 2, 1979*). For interpretation of insurance conditions with regard to exclusions of the insurer's liability, a civil law general rule that the exclusion as an exception should be interpreted restrictively (*exceptiones non sunt extendendae*) can be applied as well.

3.2.2 Trade Receivables Insured
EXPORTS AND DOMESTIC TRADE. Firstly, trade credit insurance policies cover **short-term export and/or domestic supplier credits** or trade receivables. Of course, under the conditions they were—*inter alia*—properly invoiced and declared, became due and that the outstanding debts are

within the agreed or approved insurance (revolving) limits. In addition to investment insurance, bank guarantees insurance and insurance of export credits with longer tails provided mainly by ECAs and usually underwritten on a case-by-case basis, consumer credits, etc., and some other credit risks can be insured as well. But in practice—due to unpleasant experience of the industry with some lines of insurance and lack of reinsurance capacities for nontrade risk—very few credit insurers provide insurance cover and issue **financial guarantees** that are not related to an underlying commercial transaction. Moreover, in some jurisdictions insurance does not include financial guarantees.

3.2.3 Commercial and Noncommercial Risk Insurance

COMMERCIAL AND NONCOMMERCIAL RISKS. Secondly, credit insurance policy may be limited to **commercial risk cover**, for example, to provide insurance for business conducted within the seller's own country and for their **private buyers** on OECD markets only, excluding political risk cover. By such provision of insurance cover against commercial risks and/or exclusion of political risks, the policyholders reduce the insurance premium paid, but leave public buyers, more or less trivial **noncommercial risks** and their buyers on emerging markets out of the scope of their insurance policies. It follows, that some perils such as natural disasters and political events or circumstances which directly or indirectly contributed to nonpayment or debtor's default are not covered in such a case, for example, import restrictions, general moratorium, and convertibility risk where the sum due in hard currency cannot be remitted or transferred by the debtor's bank due to foreign exchange restrictions, contract frustration, war and civil disturbances, confiscation or any other cause of *force majeure*, etc. If there is a dispute between the contract parties regarding the cause of loss, the applied **doctrine of proximate cause of loss** can help.

PUBLIC BUYERS/GUARANTORS. In addition to sovereign and subsovereign risks, the risk of the public debtors or guarantors also represents political risk. Public debtor or guarantor is usually an entity which enjoys the full faith and credit of the State or represents public authority itself, or any other public entity or institution which cannot be declared, either judicially or administratively, insolvent. But it is not always easy to classify the debtor in one or another category in practice. For assessing the status of the particular buyer, several factors are usually taken into account—that is, legal status, influence and control over the debtor, his revenues and sources of finance, and effectiveness of legal actions against the debtor—and the debtors not explicitly classified in insurance contract as public are, in principle, considered as private debtors covered by commercial risk insurance.

EXCLUSIONS. However, also in case of an effective **political risk insurance (PRI) cover**, some noncommercial risks may be excluded from cover by special insurance conditions as well, for example, terrorism, exchange rate risks, war between two or more permanent members of the United Nations Security Council, and radioactive contamination. These standard exclusions in credit insurance policies in private market are, according to practice and depending on available reinsurance capacities, generally typical risks for the exporters to bear.

Comprehensive insurance cover that embraces both commercial and noncommercial risks as displayed in Figure 3.3, and which is frequently provided under a single insurance policy with the combined general insurance conditions enclosed, is typical for whole turnover policies that provide cover also for buyers on emerging and riskier markets, for example, global whole turnover policies with commercial and noncommercial risk cover. But it may be useful for the insured to arrange a package insurance contract with comprehensive insurance coverage for his existing or desired trade pattern in some other cases too, since political risks might be important also for certain business deals in developed countries. Furthermore, it may be wise to do so

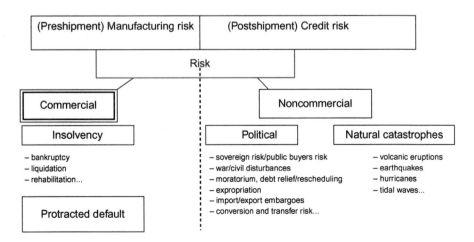

Figure 3.3 Nonpayment risks (commercial/noncommercial).

also because now in many areas we face changed circumstances and growing gray area of risks that cannot be easily categorized as either commercial or noncommercial.

Permanent insolvency of the buyer (debtor) and/or guarantor as an insured event under the commercial risk cover seems to be and should be rather straightforward reasoning to substantiate an insurance claim in case of the debtor's payment default due to bankruptcy, winding-up, etc. But in practice, depending on facts, governing national legislation and applicable insurance conditions this is not always a clear-cut case, since the debtor may be practically or effectively insolvent but not formally so (*de iure/de facto* insolvency). There should not be a problem in paying claims if the buyer's insolvency is legally ascertained and imminent and so far the insured can prove that the appointed receiver, liquidator, or administrator has agreed with the amount owed. In other cases, the claim will be paid under the condition that the debtor is forced into official insolvency proceeding or if the insurer is persuaded that the commencement of the insolvency process would not be practical, or would be ill-advised (*constructive insolvency*), for example, the debtor has disappeared or moved to an unknown address, or there is no assets available for any dividend or foreseeable result would be insufficient and in disproportion to the likely costs of the proceedings.

Insolvency is related to the buyer and is normally not extended to insolvency of his remitting bank before the transfer of monies, unless it is a guarantor or state-owned bank covered by political risk cover.

The insurer's contingent liabilities are transformed into **pending claims** when the loss-causing events occur and the risks covered materialize; such event then represents the *trigger event* to file the request for claim payment (claims under consideration) and subsequently for owed claims payment after the lapse of the waiting period.

According to general credit insurance conditions for commercial risk cover the insured event occurs, for example, with the submitted request for claims payment and evidence of the following:

- an issued final court order or decree of appointed administrator for institution of bankruptcy, receivership, rehabilitation or winding-up, or their decision on agreed debts owed;

- composition made in court proceedings for the benefit of the creditors generally;
- unsuccessfully performed execution or the levy of execution fails to satisfy the debt in full;
- 90 or 180 days have elapsed from the day the policyholder notified the insurer about overdue trade debts, or from the day of the last partial payment made in the time period from this notification.

With the insurer's consent, the debtor is deemed to be in default and the insured event may occur also, for instance, with the following:

- institution of extrajudicial composition proceeding;
- consent of all creditors to concluded out-of court settlement or valid composition arranged with all creditors;
- 90 days have lapsed away from the submission of evidence that the measures against the debtor or to commence the insolvency process would be impractical, unsuccessful, or ill-advised;
- merchandize was resold, since the risk of default had been evident and the seller—in agreement with the insurer—entered to preserver sales contract and therefore suffered actual loss due to price difference.

For the loss sustained and for the claims to be paid after the appropriate claims waiting period (CWP), if these earliest dates for indemnification after the filed request for claims payment—normally different for different insured events and established to allow the situation to correct itself—is applicable (the exception is, of course, the buyer's insolvency), the insured must timely **notify the insurer about overdue amounts** (pending claims). Due to conditional nature of the insurer's liabilities this is the insured's **essential contractual obligation**. In line with the insurance conditions, timely and properly submitted **request for claims payment** supported by the required evidence will be paid after the thorough examination and **ascertainment of loss** by the claims department. It must be proven, *inter alia*, that the insurance conditions are fulfilled and the invoiced accounts receivable are valid, within approved insurance limit and examined by the insured loss-causing events set out in the insurance policy, that is, submitted request for claims payment and required documentation must evidence these facts beyond doubt, especially that the insolvency or protracted default caused the insured loss sustained.

Protracted default, if this commercial payment default risk is covered as usual, is by definition definitely easier reasoning and basis for the insured to get claims paid. For this insured event, it is not necessary for the policyholder to submit the evidence of the debtor's insolvency. In absence of fundamental infringements of the insurance conditions, the timely notification—for example, in 45 days after the due date—of prolonged delayed payment of the buyer's previously declared, overdue and old enough outstanding debt (unpaid commercial invoice) is usually sufficient. *Ergo*, with the insurance for protracted default—under this term various risks can be subsumed—not only the buyer's payment incapability is covered but also his unwillingness to repay his due debts. Such cover is now traditionally and widely offered in credit insurance markets in addition to insolvency coverage, except perhaps sometimes for buyers in "strange" countries and difficult markets. This kind of protection is even more important for the insured seller's cash-flow management, since he may count on payments and liquidity with more certainty regardless possible complications and problems with the debt collection and insolvency proceedings. It is worth mentioning that this can be particularly important in arranging external financing with the banks.

Late payments which may be more or less customary in particular business and markets, but can be also extraordinary prolonged, are not always the result of prevailing bad habits and poor payment discipline as such or motivated by expected gains of lagging. More often they are following liquidity problems of a temporary or more permanent nature. In the latter case, they may precede, lead to, or announce the bankruptcy. Illiquidity of the companies and harsh liquidity situation in national economies may easily lead to **domino effect** which like a snowball affects numerous companies in a chain. For many sellers, delayed payments represent even bigger problems than bad debts of their insolvent buyers. Costs for reminding of such unreliable debtors (*interpellatio*), debt collection, and bridge financing needed because of induced cash-flow problems may be extremely high and thus burden business results of the companies.

PCR cover. Thirdly, if it is explicitly agreed that the insurance policy covers preshipment commercial and/or noncommercial risks, neither this cover in PCR period is not unconditional. But anyway, there are often many good reasons in trade for having such cover. If the insurer revoke or withdraw the insurance limit because the deterioration of a buyer's or country risk, the insured is usually entitled to file a preshipment risk claim. If and when the situation in the meantime improves, the buyer may claim liquidated damages and the seller will probably not be able to claim such liquidated damages from the insurer. The only cure against this is to cooperate with the insurer at early stages and to have agreed adequate *force majeure* clause in the commercial contract. Furthermore, in case of an evident and substantial deterioration of the risk after the effectiveness of the underlying contract, under certain legislation the insurer is allowed to reject the claim—also in case of a "binding contract cover" and "permanent (noncancellable) credit limits"—if the imprudent insured party nonetheless carries on with the works and dispatch. Moreover, PCR insurance rarely covers private buyer's failure to issue a letter of credit (L/C) with the exception in case of his bankruptcy and does not provide protection against the seller's own performance or completion risks and performance or insolvency risks of his subcontractors or suppliers.

PRI AND COUNTRY-COVER POLICIES. Noncommercial risk insurance policies can be structured to match different perils and may be subjected to certain specific conditions and restrictions imposed by the credit insurers' or ECAs' country-cover policies, especially for business in more difficult markets. Next to providing credit insurance cover without any special restriction and condition or being off-cover for certain business or all business in particular country and in addition to usual requirements and tied financing requirements imposed by national ECAs, one can find also some other restrictions, for example, insurance cover limited to short-term credits, higher self-retention of the insured, longer waiting period, higher insurance premium rate, and requested additional securities.

3.2.4 Claim Payment
As displayed in Figure 3.4 which illustrates the credit insurance process, if the insured event occurs and the insurance conditions are fulfilled (*condicio existit*), the insurer shall pay the claim to the policyholder or beneficiary—after the filing of the claims and claims examination—at the expiration of the waiting period, usually in 1 month after the receipt of all required documents evidencing the occurrence of the insured event and the loss amount. The claims are usually paid in the seller's or exporter's local **currency** which is legal tender in the insurer's country or in counter-value of foreign currency of the underlying commercial contract

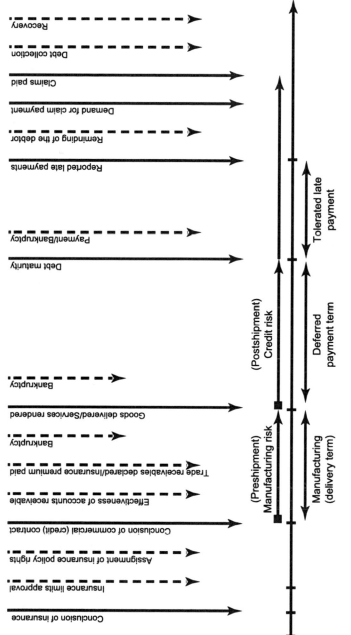

Figure 3.4 Credit insurance process.

(invoice currency), calculated, for example, by using the contractually agreed officially published exchange rate applicable at the date of the claims payment.

Provisional claims. The amount of losses incurred and accordingly reduced by the deductibles shall be indemnified to the beneficiary according to the insurance conditions and up to the insurance credit limits after the amount of loss sustained has been definitely established. Until the final amount of the loss is not known yet and if the approximate estimate of the loss is still not possible, the insurer will usually be willing to conditionally—and/or against **recourse agreement**—pay undisputable part or appropriate **provisional claim**. The insured must reimburse the insurer for any overpayment and each amount paid to which he had not been entitled including the interests thereon as of the payment day. Even in case of established and undisputable loss in claims handling procedures, the insurer may insist on the waiver of rights or policyholder's declaration of consent to claims payment and its amount.

Recourse agreement. The insurer's right to be reimbursed for any overpayment and for each claim paid to which the insured or his assignee is not entitled under the applicable insurance conditions—that is, unjust enrichment, can be assured with the recourse agreement and additional securities provided for the reimbursement commitment that may be incumbent upon them.

Subrogation. However, under general or special insurance conditions with the claims paid and up to the amount of the claims paid, the insurer is subrogated into insured creditor's rights. On the basis of governing laws, it comes to such personal subrogation *ex lege* and without the debtor's consent. To become entitled to claims payment in claims handling procedure, the insured can also transfer to the insurer his accounts receivable against the debtor or third parties (e.g., insolvency practitioner), including accessory rights, if any, by a special **assignment.** This may enable credit insurer to start and proceed with the debt collection and facilitates **recoveries** of the claims paid.

Reimbursement of costs. In addition to indemnification for losses sustained due to the debtor's payment default credit insurance also covers some other costs of the insured, excluding his own administration costs. In accordance with the insurance conditions, policyholders are entitled to reimbursement of agreed, or later approved, necessary, reasonable, and founded direct/external **costs for prevention and minimization of losses**—sometimes these expenses may be capped in practice—which are, as well as subsequent recoveries for claims paid, covered and are shared between the parties of the insurance contract proportionally to the agreed insured percentage or the insured's self-retention. The sharing of these costs is thus in favor of the insured party and with such sums successfully recovered the claims paid for losses incurred can be even increased.

3.2.5 Conditionality of Credit Insurance

Despite being excellent, very useful and efficacious financial instrument for protection against the nonpayment risks with its various functions, credit insurance is not an unconditional instrument. It requires a good deal of oversight and is subject to different sorts of insurance conditions. Apart from some already mentioned legal differences between credit insurance and other insurance contracts (see Section 2.2.3) with more obligations imposed on insured parties, credit insurance contracts usually have more conditions precedent to payment of claims and contain more exclusions of the insurers' liabilities. These conditions must be thoroughly analyzed, respected, and followed, otherwise the insured company might be exposed to risk that the claim can be rightfully rejected because of its failure to observe the terms of the insurance policy providing such breach or failure is fundamental for the insurer.

When filing the request for claims payment, the insured has to prove not only the occurrence of the insured event (credit insurance is like a "contingent guarantee") and the amount of covered financial loss as its direct consequence but also need to have a valid claim and has to comply with the laws and his obligations from the insurance contract with the attached general and/or special insurance conditions as its integral parts.

Credit insurance provides efficient protection for buyer's payment default risk but does not provide credit protection to the seller for its nonexistent or invalid trade receivables. Credit insurance does provide the creditors with the efficacious **"guarantee for reliability"** of their debtors/trade receivables (*nomen bonum*) but not also the **"guarantee for verity"** or mere existence of their accounts receivable (*nomen verum*). In brief, to be entitled to claims payment under this conditional instrument, the **insured shall dispose** *inter alia* **with a valid and unsaddled claim** toward his debtor or guarantor.

PERFORMANCE RISK. In other words, credit insurance policy, for example, does not provide protection to sellers for their own **performance risk** and does not cover their losses due to nonpayment of buyers as long as they have righteous and justifiable reason not to pay. This may be a difficult area and a bone of contention in practice as the disagreement of the contracting parties and commercial disputes are often involved. Rejections of goods may be covered as a public buyer risk, but many private credit insurers only pay such claims when the private buyer's failure arises before its insolvency. To be entitled to claims payment, the insured should fulfill his obligations from the underlying commercial contract properly and should duly complete his part of the business deal. For instance, the seller should deliver traded goods in agreed quantity and quality according to the terms and conditions of the commercial contract without legal and real defects (*peius*), or his liability should be adequately excluded. In mutual agreements with connected or reciprocal obligations of the parties, the buyer should not have an excuse or valid objections against the seller due to his nonperformance and noncompletion (*exceptio non adimpledi contractus*), or endangerment, in case of serious threat that the seller's essential obligations would not be fulfilled. Such conditions are logical as the insurer is not a party of the underlying commercial contract and has no influence on the seller's obligations toward the buyer, for example, regarding correctness of his performance in due course (identity of contracted and delivered goods (*aliud*), their quantity and quality, packing, delivery terms, handing over the shipping documents, etc.). If the claims toward the buyer is reduced because of his founded counterclaims (set-offs, etc.), as the outcome the claims payment for the indemnification of the insured is proportionally reduced as well. Requirement of an existing, valid, and unencumbered buyer's unsettled debts witnesses and represents one important aspect of conditional nature of credit insurance policy and the insurer's liability. The contracts therefore should not be unlawful and insured accounts receivable should not be null and void because of an absolute impossibility of completion, subject matter of an underlying commercial contract should not be undetermined or indefinable, the contract shall have permissible *causa* ("approximate equivalent" of *consideration* from the legal systems based on Common Law) and must be concluded in correct form, if prescribed by the applicable laws, contract terms should come to their expiration and deferred conditions should be accomplished, etc.

●●●

Credit insurance policy covers buyer's payment default risk but not the seller's performance risk.

Surety Bonds

Seller's or contractor's performance risk can be covered by **service/supply bank guarantees** which are normally unconditional and independent from underlying contracts and are *grosso modo* issued on simple or first demand of the beneficiaries as well as by **contract surety bonds**, especially performance, maintenance, and retention bonds.

Despite the latter, undertakings are included in credit insurance class in a broader sense and can be issued also by credit insurers or ECAs, suretyship is quite different animal. One may say it is a credit guarantee and not insurance. These financial instruments are usually issued by the surety companies in favor of the beneficiaries—obligees (buyers or employers) pursuant to which the sureties guarantee performance of another party of an obligation and undertake on default of the debtors—primary obligors (the principals) to compensate them for damages up to the bond amounts, or to perform or execute the underlying contracts or any contractual obligation. On the other hand, credit insurer assumes nonpayment risk and undertakes to make claims payment to the insured creditor (seller) on payment default of his debtor (buyer), that is, the third party, upon occurrence of the specified insured event.

The liability of surety is normally—unlike on-demand bank guarantees—conditional, default-based, accessory, and coextensive with the main debtor's (obligor's) primary obligations from the underlying commercial contract. From this point of view both—credit insurance policies and surety bonds—follow the principle of indemnity and do represent conditional obligations of their issuers, but the former are by the rule discreet and stand-alone and are not subordinated to another contract. Although a surety bond may be issued by the insurance company, it is in a strict sense not an insurance contract, that is, bilateral agreement to indemnify the insured against loss incurred if the insured event—debtor's insolvency or protracted default—occurs. On the contrary, a contract surety bond is more a contract guarantee than insurance (the risk in suretyship is the seller and not the buyer!), it is not discreet and is often even three-party agreement (*contractus multilaterales*) pursuant to which the surety assumes a secondary liability to the beneficiary for the default of the contractor/seller. Unlike in credit insurance where the seller (creditor) is the insured party, the seller/contractor acts as the principal for issuing of the performance bond and he is the one who pays insurance premium and fees, but the claims are paid to the beneficiary (the buyer/employer). Therefore, in bonding payment of insurance premium and compliance with insurance conditions consequently have not such crucial impact to termination of contract and claims payment as they have in credit insurance.

Moreover, in bonding and credit insurance terminology and the wording of the contracts often differ, rights of recourse to the insured or to the principal differ as well, surety bonds are frequently issued also indirectly (fronting), while the underwriting in bonding is also rather specific and may include collateral.

BANK GUARANTEES AND UNFAIR CALLING. Payment bank guarantees and other bank instruments are sometimes complements and also substitutes for credit insurance, especially for specific insurance policy and mainly cover individual business transactions with longer terms. These instruments are frequently used worldwide and in parallel to provide guarantees for both commercial contract counterparties. Credit insured sellers are thus frequently bound to provide to their buyers, for example, tender, performance/maintenance, retention, and repayment bonds or guarantees. Because these on-demand undertakings are predominantly unconditional (pay first, argue later!) with the guarantor's original, primary, and independent liability, they make their principals (main obligors) exposed to inherent **unfair calling risk** and abusive or fraudulent, but otherwise complying, demands of their buyers (beneficiaries), that is, where a bank honors the guarantee notwithstanding that the beneficiary is not entitled to be paid since the main debtor—who must reimburse the paying bank—is not in breach of its obligations in the underlying commercial transaction.

Bond call insurance cover can be obtained for the risk of the unfair calling of on-demand guarantees. Such insurance can be provided by credit insurers and ECAs—also in addition to credit insurance cover and rarely on a stand-alone basis—against the guarantees being called unfairly by private or public buyers/employers, including so called fair callings that arise from political and other noncommercial risks that have frustrated underlying commercial contract.

●●●

Credit insurance cannot make a bad commercial contract good.

UNDERLYING CONTRACT. Conditional nature of credit insurers' obligations and their "accessory" but stand-alone link with the debtor's liability can put a paramount importance of the **underlying commercial contract** in focus of the claims handling procedure. Commercial contract can have a crucial effect on claims payment, when the claim shall be paid, or even whether the claim shall be paid at all and to what extent. This is especially true for the **contract delivery and payment terms** which must be clear and unambiguous as much as possible. Furthermore, contract payment terms must not exceed the maximum credit period agreed and prescribed by applicable insurance conditions. Credit insurance provides protection against the "wrongfully chosen" buyer and his non-payments, but unlike independent and unconditional on-demand bank guarantees or stand-by L/C *per se* cannot prevent or cure all possible deficiencies of the underlying commercial contract and its bad or unfavorable wording for the seller. Insurers often say that their credit insurance policies cannot make a bad commercial contract good and that their credit insurance policies can only be as good as the underlying contracts. The principle of indemnity leads the purpose of credit insurance to provide protection and to place the insured in the same position as if he has suffered no loss and nothing more.

Despite wishful thinking some events or losses are thus not covered by credit insurance. Already at first sight it is clear that the payment terms based on acceptance of goods and services by the customer, for example, in his country, give rise to the risks of exporters and hinder them to demonstrate to their insurers that they had not been paid; therefore, the buyer's acceptance of the goods must be clearly stipulated in the contract. Because, in general, transport risks and cargo losses are not covered under the credit insurance policy but can be insured separately, it is *inter alia* important who is responsible for the carriage of goods and insurance and one has to bear in mind applied ICC Incoterms 2010 clauses (ICC Publication No. 715) and their variations, for example, if the buyer's payments are contingent upon delivery by using trade terms FOB, CIF, etc. Since under the credit insurance, the cancellation of an import/export license or its nonrenewal, nor the failure to obtain it, can be covered, it is also important whose responsibility is to obtain an export/import license. And last but not least, it is also important what the contract and/or applicable laws say about the place of payment. For an insurance policy to cover transfer risk, it is required that it is incumbent on the importer to effect payment outside his country. Should the place of payment be in the debtor's country, the debtor shall be deemed to have fulfilled his obligations by payment in his country and any hindrance for transfer of thus paid amounts out of the country will normally not be covered.

●●●
_____

Credit insurance policy can only be as good as the underlying contract.
_____

COMMERCIAL DISPUTES. If the seller has not performed or completed his contractual obligations, he cannot be able to establish a debt due to him and a valid claim. As long as there is a continuing or documented dispute between the parties of the underlying contract, unless the buyer's objections are manifestly baseless, the insurers will most probably defer admitting liabilities (*condicio pendet*) until the buyer's liability has been established to their satisfaction and the dispute has been resolved in the creditor's favor by a (final/enforceable) decision, whether arbitrated or judicial. This can be also witnessed by the buyer's objections given after reasonable time for reclamations, by independent report from a surveyor in favor of the seller, by receiving several similar reports of disputes from other companies at the same time witnessing spurious disputes or frivolous complaints—for example, an excuse for nonpayment or chicanery to decrease contract price—without any good reason just to blackmail and to avoid effecting payments, or by arbitration or judicial settlement of disputes. Such overdue payments and buyer's reclamations and objections, including his counterclaims, offer to return the goods, as well as his proposals to decrease contract price, extend payment terms or proposals for rescheduling the debts, should be reported to the insurer. He will then decide on a case-by-case basis if the dispute is genuine and whether to proceed with adjudication, arbitration, and court procedures or other debt collection activities and measures.

By submitting the request for claims payment, it is assumed that the debtor is insolvent and that means the insured has to discontinue the deliveries and stop trading with him, unless under the different agreement with the insurer or his instructions and with agreed sharing of the income with the insurer as salvage. To establish and ascertain claim, it can be therefore important to have adequate clauses for ex post settlement of disputes stipulated in the commercial contract, for example, governing law and binding and enforceable arbitration clauses (arbitrium) regarding forum, arbitrators, procedure, and language of procedure in *neutral* country, etc.

●●●
_____

Credit insurance has a *nomen bonum* and not a *nomen verum* effect.
_____

Credit insurance provides guarantee for creditworthiness of the debtors (*nomen bonum*) and not also the guarantee for the existence, validity, and enforceability of creditor's rights (*nomen verum*). As for assignments of accounts receivable in civil law provisions, the latter guarantee is given only if explicitly agreed. As already said, in light of the principles of indemnity and prohibition of unjust enrichment, the insured must reimburse the insurer for any overpayment and for each amount of claims paid to which he is not being entitled. You cannot have a cake and eat it too. This insurer's **right of recourse** against the insured, for example, in case of an assignment of insurance policy rights to the lending bank, can be additionally assured with the recourse agreement and given collateral. Without a valid claim in case of his failure to fulfill his own obligations from the underlying contract, the enriched insured has no legal basis for indemnification; the seller's nonperformance, videlicet, has crucial effect on the risks and his counterparty's payment obligations. One may even say that due to his failure to fulfill his obligations from the underlying commercial contract, the subject matter of credit insurance—that is, his trade receivables—would be defective as much as the essential element of the risk underwritten, that is, uncertainty, would be missing. It could be even expected in such cases with certainty that the loss will be incurred, since such "debt" most probably would not be paid by the buyer.

DOCUMENTATION RISK. For many credit insurers and ECAs their traditional policy is that they do not accept any documentation risk and that the insured parties and their banks remain responsible for their own documents such as, for instance, bills of exchange (B/E) or promissory notes, requested corporate or bank guarantees, and ROT clauses. These undertakings and documents, even if submitted, will normally not be examined or approved by the underwriter prior to claims handling procedure, and if the loss arises because a failure in such documents, the request for claim payment would be most probably rejected. Thus, the claim is normally not payable if the underlying or submitted documents are faulty, incomplete, invalid, or enforceable.

Anyway, the documentation risk might be a tricky practical issue, especially in medium-term export credit and investment insurance, since very important documentation in this kind of deals may be complex, demanding, and untested in applicable legal framework.

Despite the credit insurer underwrites buyers' and not sellers' risks, the insurance company does not evaluate and assess the buyers' risks only, but, on the other hand, does not neglect creditworthiness, financial, technical, and other capabilities of his clients and their associated performance risks.

3.2.6 Obligations of the Insured

Another important aspect and reflection of a conditional nature of credit insurance are stemming from the **insured's obligations** from his insurance policy and insurance conditions. In order not to have the claim rejected, it is of a paramount importance for the insured company to observe all sorts of general and special insurance conditions, that is, *inter alia*,

1. to inform the insurer promptly and with due care about the relevant facts and circumstances that may influence the risks, their underwriting, and credit risk management;
2. to obtain and maintain required (import/export) licenses and to comply with the laws and regulations, including the laws of the buyer's country;
3. to refrain from *overloading*, to change the payment terms and conditions and to waive creditor's rights against the debtor without the insurer's consent;
4. to regularly and promptly declare all outstanding and covered debts;
5. to notify the insurer without delay the circumstances indicating that the debtor is experiencing financial difficulties, payment default, and untolerated delays;
6. to stop with subsequent supplies to such debtors and to take all reasonable measures to prevent and minimize loss;
7. to file requests for claims payment and required evidence of the occurrence of the insured event and of the loss sustained in due time; and
8. to pay invoiced and owed insurance premium, etc.

Only strict **compliance with the fundamental insurance policy terms and conditions** makes the insured to avoid pitfalls and guarantees the claims payment in full after the occurrence of the insured event. It is not advisable to count on claims paid for which no liability exists, and neither on *ex gratia* claims payment, despite the insurer would normally like to retain his long-term cooperation with the insured to the satisfaction of both business partners. On the other hand, reinsurers may need not *follow the fortunes* of the primary insurers to pay for a loss that is not covered by the underlying insurance contract (see, e.g., *St. Paul Fire & Marine Company v. Morice (1906), 22 T.L.R. 449, American Ins. Co. v. North Am. Co. for Property and Casualty Ins., 697 F. 2d. 79 (2d Cir. 1982), Insurance Company of North America v. US Fire Insurance Company (348 N.Y.S. 2d 122 (N.Y. App. Div. 1973), etc.).* Definitely, fatal or too big failures or serious infringements of policyholders and their repetitions cannot be tolerated.

●●●
___

Credit insurance policy is useful and efficacious but conditional financial instrument.

___

INSURANCE DECLARATIONS. The insured has to submit **insurance declarations** regularly, normally on a monthly basis for a previous month, with the complete specification of all (new) outstanding debts of his buyers insured with their amounts and payment terms. Invoiced **insurance premium** for credit insurance coverage is then calculated on the basis of reported actual turnover of the insured or weighted average balance of outstanding debts owed to him.

Timely submitted complete insurance declaration is fundamental contractual obligation of the insured. For **underdeclaration**—this is a problem for many credit insurers—the insurer will subsequently charge additional premium and the omission of this duty leads to another repercussion that such **nonreported credits are not covered**. On the other hand, in credit insurance also the **due payment of insurance premium** and other charges is, unlike for some other insurance types, a **condition precedent to claims payment**. The insured has no valid or fully effective claim if the premium owed is not paid in accordance with general and special insurance conditions. In the event of a breach of any condition precedent, the insurer normally also has the right to retain any insurance premium already paid.

DUE DILIGENCE. As already said, according to insurance conditions the infringement of certain other duties and obligations of the insured may also have rigorous implications on (in)validity and none-ffectiveness of credit insurance coverage and/or may constitute grounds to terminate the insurance contract, probably with the retention of (minimum) insurance premium paid or owed. Therefore, **the insured must observe his duties and has to manage his credit insurance policy with due care and diligence**.

PREVENTION AND MINIMIZATION OF LOSSES. Apart from mentioned obligations to disclose requested data and facts as well as to inform the insurer about the specific circumstances with the possible impact to risks underwritten before the issuance of the insurance policy, the insured must also immediately report all such changed circumstances and has to act as a prudent trader during the whole insurance period. He must exercise such reasonable care and prudence as a reasonable seller would exercise in the business transaction of the same kind. The omission to report information being material to the insurer's perception of the risks underwritten, for example, unfavorable trading history, is a common reason for credit insurers to reject claims. That means, **the insured has to act with due care and as he is not insured** to promptly respond to external circumstances with all required **reasonable and practicable measures to prevent the loss-causing events or to minimize their possibilities to occur as well as to minimize the amount of loss incurred**. In these processes he must do his best and act in commercially sensible way, he needs to cooperate with the insurer and has to follow his instructions. To enable the insurer to prevent and minimize losses and to use such information as a risk indicator for other insured sellers, the insured has to report any overdue payments—for example, at the expiry of the maximum extension period—as well as other circumstances likely to aggravate the nonpayment risk underwritten.

DEBT COLLECTION. On the other hand and *vis-à-vis* his debtor, the insured has to, for example, remind the buyer on his overdue debts, he must preserve and assert his rights as well as maintain and exercise or enforce given securities, that is, to protest the unpaid or nonaccepted B/E in accordance with applicable laws, to institute court and execution proceedings, and so forth. Moreover, without the insurer's consent the insured should not recognize the debtor's counterclaim and is obliged not to enter into any settlements, compositions, or compounds relating to trade receivables insured, nor can waive and assign his rights thereof. The insured has to start also with other **debt collection** activities on time and has to carry them out with due care and in agreement—if possible prior to such activities—with the insurer. In particular, the insured should not, unless otherwise agreed with the insurer, increase his exposure to unreliable buyer who is late with due payments in excess of tolerated usual delays, for example, **prohibition of imprudent trading** and *overtrading*. In failure regarding these duties, such deliveries, as well as deliveries to a particular buyer above the insurance limit, are not covered, and the insured is not entitled for such claims payments or the amount of claims paid can be reduced, even for losses arising out of other credits/deliveries. In addition, without the insurer's consent—which is usually not withheld unreasonably—the insured seller should not prolong agreed payment terms and grant discounts, rebates, and bonuses, he must inform the insurer about such requests and reclamations of the buyer as well as about his demands for partial payments. Reasonable **costs** of the insured for such loss prevention and minimization activities performed in consent with the insurer are reimbursed to him at the same proportion as the claims paid for the loss sustained, irrespective of the success of these measures.

CLAIM PAYMENT. Finally, if such measures do not bear fruit, the insured must file **request for claims payment** with the prescribed complete documentation, and this must be done within specified period of time from the due date. Failure to make claim within the required timescale usually allows the insurer to reject claim payment; nevertheless, the insurer is bound by similar reinsurance conditions. It is also worth mentioning for the conclusion that commercial risk credit insurance policy normally does not cover fraud and the insurer shall be released from his obligations to pay claim if the insured party or persons from his sphere violate laws and regulations in force.

RECOVERY. Even after the claims payment, the insured must follow the insurer's instructions and guidelines and has to cooperate with the insurer—who may be subrogated to the insured creditor's rights, takes them over by the assignment or is appointed as an agent or attorney—to get from the debtor and/or his guarantor as much **recoveries** as possible. Recovered amounts must be remitted to insurer and are shared between the parties of the insurance contract in accordance with the agreed insured percentage.

3.2.7 Percentage of Cover

To avoid moral hazard and to stimulate the insured party to cooperate with the insurer in debt collection, insurance conditions stipulate the obligation for the insurer to indemnify the insured for overdue outstanding debts of his debtors within their insurance limits, if the loss is incurred as a direct consequence of the occurrence of the insured event, up to the agreed **insured percentage**.

The liability of the insurer is therefore limited with the approved credit limits for covered trade receivables and is computed on the basis of previously properly declared invoice value of unpaid deliveries, including freight and insurance costs and with typically excluded agents' commissions; they are usually not paid unless the customer pays in full. The claims paid thus compensate the insured seller for major part of direct material loss arising from debtor's insolvency or protracted default and comprise the debtor's regular payment obligations—insured principal amount of the overdue debt (VAT might be a special issue), while the discounts and bonuses, default interests, liquidated damages, penalties, and suchlike are normally not covered under the credit insurance.

Currency fluctuations. Credit insurance does not cover losses due to **exchange rate risk**. Credit insurance cover is usually provided in domestic currency or in currency used for the insured's financial accounts. When the commercial contract is denominated in foreign currency, for the counter-value of the claims paid published official exchange rates relating to the invoice date of payment (or effective date of the underlying commercial contract for PCR insurance), or claims payment dates, are usually used. By arranging insurance cover in the currency of the commercial contract, this part of the exchange rate risk associated with the credit insurance can be eliminated for the exporter.

INSURED'S SELF-RETENTION. Last but not least, claims paid are compensation for the loss sustained, but in credit insurance (proportional insurance coverage), the sum insured is normally reduced by the insured's **self-retention** as a "deductible" which has to be borne by the insured seller himself. As already said, short-term credit insurance against commercial risks has standard self-retention rate of near 10 percent which can be higher for certain buyers or buyers in difficult markets. On the other hand, especially for political risks insurance this rate can be even lower with its reciprocal value, that is, the percentafe of cover (PC) of 90 and up to 100 percent, for example, if the lending bank is the beneficiary under the policy. These percentages may be different in practice depending on quality of the insured risk portfolio or for specific credit limits, and, of course, in case of nonproportional insurance coverage.

Prohibition of multiple insurances. Uninsured amounts or excess risk which is not covered with the claim paid should be normally borne by the insured himself and this residual risk should not be additionally/ separately insured or unilaterally transferred elsewhere, unless agreed otherwise (e.g., for transfer the excess risk to mother company or to sub- or main contractor). Many laws do not allow double and multiple insurances for the same risk, interest, and time, and prescribe that the insured can only claim once or proportional part of the loss incurred, even he has several insurance policies covering the same loss on property. On the other hand, credit insurance policies typically go even further and stipulate that the credit insurance claim would be paid only after and above the payments of claims from other insurances, for example, from marine and liability insurances (or proceeds from realization of guarantees and other securities).

When the bank guarantee or surety bond is required as a condition for insurance cover, the loss normally shall not be ascertained until a final judgment for the amount owing has been obtained against the guarantor.

IML. There may be additional limitation to overall claims paid quite often imposed by the credit insurance conditions, that is, the **insurer's maximum liability (IML)** with the capped aggregate maximum amount of claims payable during the credit insurance policy period, mostly defined on the basis of the paid annual insurance premium.

CHAPTER 4

Risk Management and Credit Insurance

4.1 INTEGRAL AND CREDIT RISK MANAGEMENT

In a highly competitive, demanding, and turbulent contemporary business environment, various business risks in local and global markets as

Credit Insurance. DOI: http://dx.doi.org/10.1016/B978-0-12-411458-6.00004-6

impetus nowadays push the companies to devote particular attention to **risk management** in order to achieve long-term competitiveness and desired business results. Nonexistent or ineffective risk management may easily lead to recorded losses in a particular business transaction as well as in company's overall operations. Risks may well diminish profitability, increase losses and as a consequence lead to illiquidity, reduce the capital and threaten solvency of the company and finally may bring its operations to a halt.

In a traditional manner, predominately risk ignoring and risk averse companies considered and managed risk with the *ex post* reactions after the occurrence of the risk, simple risk mitigation techniques and instruments were applied *ad hoc* for each or only for few bigger individual business transactions and were mainly focused on financial risks.

INTEGRAL RISK MANAGEMENT. Nowadays, risk management is turned to be a process whereby companies methodically address the risks attached to their business activities with the goal of achieving sustained benefits, that is, course of action taken to assess and monitor the risks and company's exposures, to protect themselves against the risks or mitigate the risks and to reduce or minimize their consequences and adverse effects on company's operations for the purpose of increasing the companies' value to their stakeholders. Good companies begin to apply a holistic view and are reoriented from individual business transactions to comprehensive analysis and active risk management on a risk portfolio basis and put risk management system and activities in the focus of financial management of the company.

By **integral risk management**, with **active credit risk portfolio management** included, the companies with advanced analytical deterministic and stochastic models assess, quantify and monitor their risk exposure and proactively mitigate the risks in accordance with their capacities and financial and business strategy bearing in mind, *inter alia*, their business goals, actual and future risks, existing and desired risk portfolio as well as protection techniques, devices and instruments, their effects, availability, and costs. This discipline and one of the foremost modern methodological business processes comprise numerous business functions on various management levels and is reflected in organizational structure, defined roles and responsibilities, information flows and even in changed business culture in the company. Apart from goals to efficiently protect the company against the risks, including concentration risk, risk management system applied can serve additional profit goals and goals to ensure that the operations of the company are running in compliance with the laws and requirements of the regulators, etc. Risk management is attended to secure financial and business efficiency and simultaneously to ensure appropriate level of economic security. Active risk management regularly assesses transactions, operations and risk portfolio, ensures compliance of operations with the laws and regulations, with the demand and requirements of the customers, competitiveness of the offer, capital adequacy standards and with the risk adjusted yields. Moreover, risk management operations can contribute to generation of additional income and the risk management department may even act as a profit center in the company.

Nowadays risk management on strategic, tactical, and operational level does not comprise only:

i. developed IS and appropriate organizational structure, division of labor and responsibilities (separated business functions of sales, risk assessment, risk management, and control is usually recommended),
ii. identification of the risks (risk inventory and risk profile),
iii. risk analysis and assessment regarding different risks, type of loss, its amount and probability,
iv. analysis of risk exposures and their likely trends,
v. risk monitoring,
vi. internal and external reporting and control,

but it is also oriented toward the identification and evaluation of various methods, techniques, devices, and instruments for protection. This also includes the analysis of their use and effects, advantages and disadvantages, their availability, prices or costs and benefits as well as other terms and conditions. The companies include various economic, financial and legal instruments and their combinations, also very sophisticated ones, in their day-to-day operations and activities in accordance with their risk management strategy and policies. All these are intended to perform risk management activities cost-effectively in line with company's business strategy and goals, know-how and other capacities available and with the aim to ensure adequate economic safety, desired financial effects and other positive impacts.

ORGANIZATIONAL ISSUES. Risk management can be organized in independent coordination unit or department with the appointed risk manager directly reporting to the top management, but can also be part of the financial department or elsewhere where certain risks appear. Because trade receivables usually represent important part of companies' assets, credit risks jeopardize their business results and can seriously harm the finances of the companies. Therefore, consistent and active credit risk management can be of a paramount importance for the company, its business success and existence.

●●●

Any safeguard measure including insurance is usually better than none.

CREDIT RISK MANAGEMENT. Credit insurance provides useful protection tool against very important payment default risks. In addition to pure insurance under competitive conditions which is limited to financial cover only and is arising from its curative and active function, risk management of the companies can also enjoy additional benefits from outsourcing of certain functions and auxiliary services of credit insurance, that is, credit information, risk monitoring, debt collection and other business, financial and legal consulting within the **serviced credit insurance**. These supplementary services may increase clients' loyalty and create value added for the insured companies and, on the other hand, make credit insurers able to complement and complete their supply of services and products as well as to achieve synergy effects. Moreover, nowadays some credit insurers try to develop and offer even more comprehensive credit services combining credit insurance with other lines, such as transport and legal costs insurances, extended to logistics, invoicing and financial solutions by merging them into one product covering more or less all problems related to trade.

To have credit insurance in place can be convenient and important step in development of (credit) risk management of the company. For this, one does not need to wait first to develop all of the risk management functions in the company completely. Nevertheless, it is all about the (r)evolution, like in biology (history). Risk management system development is gradual and usually step-by-step process with the ongoing learning process and is becoming more and more computerized and sophisticated, especially in large companies and financial institutions.

●●●———

Credit insurance cannot substitute the company's own credit risk management, but can be its useful and efficacious complement.

——

Bad risk management and poor credit management definitely influence the insurer's appetite for the risks offered or transferred. It may even lead to rejection or revocation of insurance cover, to imposed restrictions and limitations, or at least to a higher pricing and other less-advantageous insurance conditions.

Figure 4.1 illustrates integral risk management with (serviced) credit insurance as one of efficacious protection devices used for credit risk management of the companies that sell their products on deferred payment terms.

4.2 HOW TO OBTAIN A CREDIT INSURANCE POLICY

4.2.1 Insured Parties

Practically each company which sells goods and/or renders services on credit or deferred payment terms and would like to offer this possibility to its customers to improve its competitiveness and increase sales, can insure its short-term trade receivables of its domestic and/or foreign buyers with the insurance company which provides credit insurance services.

It is not always necessary that the contracting party of the credit insurance contract is the same person who has his legal and pecuniary interest insured and is also entitled to claims payment for the loss incurred upon the occurrence of the insured event and after the lapse of the waiting period (**the insured**). The **existence of pecuniary interest** not to bear financial loss or to ensure economic safety against possible damages or losses on the subject matter of the insurance, that is, accounts receivable, is an essential condition for conclusion of an insurance contract and *causa* of this contractual relationship. In such a case in property insurance we talk about the **insurable interest**. Because of this insurable interest the insurance contract differs from other contracts where performance and fulfillment of obligations are of an aleatory nature. In the opposite case of a nonexistent insurable interest (absence of *causa*) the insurance could be abused and used for the

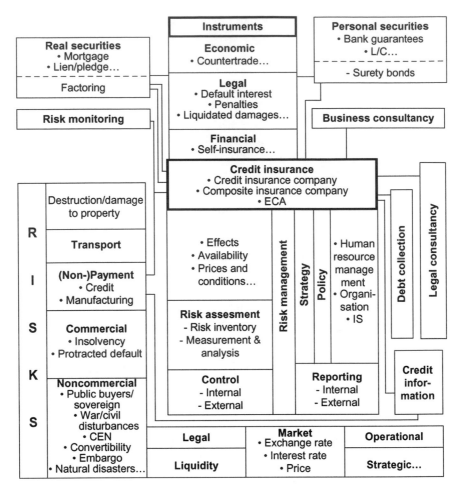

Figure 4.1 Risks, risk management, and (serviced) credit insurance.

purposes not suitable for the insurance. On the other hand, the existence of insurable interest is indispensable but not sufficient, for example, fraudsters can have the same profane interest. Beneficial interest need to be possible and legitimate, legally permissible and must not contravene legal and public order *(contra legem)*, that is, it has to be eligible for legal protection.

As already said, at least in principle the contracting party who concludes the insurance contract and **the insured** (the beneficiary of the insurance policy or the loss payee) may not always be the same person when the insurance is concluded on someone else's account or to account to whom the insurance refers.

A contracting party that is not the insured may have the obligations from the insurance contract, for example, the payment of insurance premium, but not also the rights against the insurer. He directly does not have the insurable interest to be insured against the risks which are contractual *causa* for the insured party. The third person (beneficiary/ loss payee) whose pecuniary interest is insured with the insurance contract concluded for the third person's account becomes entitled under the loss-payable clause of the insurance contract upon his consent. With his accession to insurance contract and in addition to the rights of the insurance contract taken over, the insured assumes also the obligations related to his rights.

In credit insurance, the contracting party who concludes the insurance contract and the insured are rarely different persons, for example, a mother company for the account of its insured or coinsured daughter companies. Apart from companies, the sellers or exporters, in credit insurance the insured parties can also be banks and factors to whom the trade receivables were assigned. Because in credit insurance it is an essential contractual obligation of the insured to report the insurer all material facts that may influence the risks of his buyers and as the seller is their partner in underlying transactions, the credit insurance contract for the third party's account will be seldom concluded in practice.

Assignment of insurance policy rights. Distinctly, in credit insurance practice it is often talked about the **beneficiary** under the insurance policy or the **loss payee** together with the assignment of the insurance policy rights to lending banks and other financiers, or this entitled person can also be "the bankrupt's estate" represented by insolvency practitioner.

It is required also for the beneficiary to have legally admissible pecuniary interest that the insured event does not occur at the time of his filing of the claim and the claims payment. Assignor of the insured accounts receivable does not have such interest (anymore), except, for example, in case of recourse factoring. For the assignment or encumbrance of trade receivables prior consent of the insurer is always required for the validity of insurance coverage and the rights from the credit insurance contracts are never assigned or transferred to assignees automatically. Credit insurance contract is concluded between the contracting parties and with the entering of a new contracting party in underlying commercial or credit relations the risks underwritten can be fundamentally and materially changed. With the assignment of trade receivables the risks could worsen, probability for loss-causing event can increase and possibilities for loss prevention and minimization measures, for debt collection and recovery can be diminished.

Umbrella insurance policies. The **group of companies** can also conclude a (collective) credit insurance contract, for example, a holding company for its all or several particular daughter companies. In such a case we usually have a framework credit insurance contract concluded with the holding company and several individual supplementary contracts with daughter companies. Instead of otherwise prevailing individual insurance policies in credit insurance one can find umbrella insurance policies for affiliated companies as well. These companies within a group usually centralize or coordinate their credit risk management and are thus able to offer bigger volume of business insured and more dispersed risk portfolio to their insurers. Therefore, they may benefit from lower premium rates and better insurance conditions.

KNOW-HOW. It is recommended for the companies, their managers, and officers to be acquainted with the insurance conditions, possibilities and advantages to be gained from the credit insurance policy and its impact on the whole business, and credit risk management. It is important for them to consider and to comply with the terms of the insurance policy, credit limits and applicable general insurance conditions. Useful information can be gathered from Internet and underwriters—(future) guardians of the insurance policies as well as from experienced specialized credit insurance **brokers** and other **consultants**. To get the most from the credit insurance they can be included in the process from the scratch, from initial strategy development, comparing and selecting the most appropriate cover, training of the staff and insurance policy operations, renewals, claims handling, etc.

4.2.2 Request for Insurance

Because credit insurance services and their supportive terms and conditions are usually flexibly individualized and tailored to specific needs of the insured parties, the first step for the conclusion of an insurance contract and long-term relations between the parties is the submission of the proposal or **request for insurance** with the filled-in **questionnaire** (application) form.

Detailed questionnaire contains all required information about the company and its business needed for the insurer to prepare his credit insurance offer *(oferta)*. The request and submitted data of the insured and his business are always treated as **confidential information** and may be later on attached to insurance policy as its integral part.

The request for insurance contains **general information** about the company (the insured) and the **sales** in his ordinary course of business, his annual turnover per countries and its dynamics, for example, seasonal sales of particular products, envisaged future sales to foreign and domestic customers, especially those with larger volume of trade. To avoid any ambiguity it is of a particular importance to indicate clearly full and correct firm, seat and address of the buyer's registered office with its registration or official identification numbers, especially if the insurance limits are requested for several affiliated companies and for the companies with the similar firms. This caveat might be important to avoid nasty surprise and unpleasant situation that the credits to particular buyers would not have been covered because of mistakes regarding wrongfully submitted data and information. Any changes of this data in the insurance contract period shall be regularly and promptly notified to the insurer.

The insured must give the true and accurate information regarding his volume of trade and its spread including his estimation on his insured future sales to particular buyers and **has to disclose his trading history and payment experience**, especially unsatisfactorily experiences with nonpayments, delayed payments, average delays, and the amounts of overdue debts of his individual buyers, etc.

The questionnaire also comprises columns with credit and **payment terms and conditions** including payment methods, contractual and actual terms of payment for particular customers, information on company's **credit risk management** and ordinary checking of the buyers' **creditworthiness**, given **securities**, for example, ROT clauses, and **debt collection** methods and practice of the insured, etc.

In their risk assessment and examination of the risk portfolio offered for insurance underwriters examine and assess:

 i. nature of the business insured, countries and branches of buyers;
ii. volume and spread of trade;

iii. creditworthiness and other credit information on buyers and other companies in the group, if any;
iv. previous trading and payment experience of the insured;
v. business policy and practice of crediting and credit risk management of the insured.

Because a credit insurer takes over from the insured his buyers' payment default risks, the insurer who has to do his business successfully and wants to apply efficacious risk management must be acquainted with information, facts, and circumstances that may influence the risks underwritten. Full **disclosure of all relevant facts and circumstances** with due care of the insured and in accordance with the principle of good faith as well as immediate notification of any worrying or relevant changed circumstances or event likely to cause a loss—of which the insured is aware of (or should be aware of) and except those already known for the insurer or generally known—which might influence the risk assessment and the insurer's decisions to underwrite risks and conclude insurance contract, to approve insurance limits and prescribe insurance conditions as well as to perform debt collection activities, if necessary, is **essential contractual obligation of the insured**. As already said, validity of insurance cover and claims payment are conditional upon the insured's proper performance of his disclosure and reporting duties. Any misrepresentation, nondisclosure or false disclosure, concealed material facts and circumstances, deliberately or by negligence, can have a dramatic effect and may lead to nonpayment of claim in case of occurrence of the insured event, that is, buyer's insolvency or protracted default. Companies are usually in close and long-lasting relations with their buyers and thus know them well. Such information important for underwriting and risk management therefore needs to be shared with the long-term business partner, that is, credit insurance company who collects insurance premiums for the risks underwritten and provides credit insurance cover for the insured companies.

●●●──

Credit insurers and insured parties are long-term business partners professionally cooperating on the basis of mutual trust in accordance with the principle of good faith.

Moreover, credit insurance contract is a contract *uberrimae fidei* where even more, that is, **utmost good faith**, is required. Both parties of the insurance contract must act in good faith even before the conclusion of an insurance contract when the insured has to disclose and report all material facts and circumstances which influence or might influence the risks underwritten.

4.2.3 Buyers' Insurance Limits

In addition to the mentioned filled-out general questionnaire before the conclusion of the insurance contract the company, (the insured) has to submit also the **request for approval of insurance limit** for each of his buyers he intends to insure. These limits on buyers represent the amounts of trade receivables a credit insurer has committed to cover.

INSURANCE LIMIT REQUEST. These credit limit requests contain several questions and columns, for example, name and seat of the buyer, his ownership structure, and other identification data including the statement whether the buyer is unknown or known with the specification of previous payments:

- payment record—is the buyer good or bad debtor/payer;
- credit periods (in number of days between the date of invoice and due date) with the explanation when the debts are created—for example, on dispatch or completion, and described contract **payment terms and conditions** including requested securities, if any;
- previous eventual late payments, for example, in the last year;
- goods delivered and/or services rendered;
- annual sales turnover with the values and dynamics of deliveries;
- (average) **outstanding debts**;
- any other information which may influence the risk assessment.

ADEQUATE INSURANCE LIMITS. It is very important for companies to make realistic estimation of their possibilities and **forecasted volume of trade** with their buyers for the period ahead as well as **its maximum and accumulated outstanding debts of their particular buyers**. Bearing in mind these estimations and buyers' creditworthiness, this can be a good basis for suggesting or **requesting adequate and appropriate credit insurance limits**. These limits are usually **revolving** in short-term credit insurance business set on rollover basis and are valid for more than one delivery and for several commercial contracts, that is, once the goods are delivered and paid for, set credit insurance limit is freed up for subsequent deliveries. As PCR cover is related to costs of the insured and not to the invoice value, these insurance limits may be lower than insurance limits for the same buyers for postshipment credit risk cover. The insurer will only pay claims up to the amount of the set insurance limits. Therefore, the insured has to ensure that the suggested credit limits are sufficient to cover aggregate contract price of all invoices expected to be outstanding at one time.

Approved and not used or not enough utilized insurance limits may adversely diminish the insurance capacities available for other companies and may lead to decrease of such limits in future. At the next time renewals insurance limits most probably would not be extended if the insured for a longer period of time have not made business with such buyer. If a **minimum and deposit insurance premium** is agreed, it may also happen that the insured has to pay additional premium for the unutilized limit that reflects the ratios of approved and used limits or expected and actually invoiced insurance premium.

Regarding the concentration of the insured's trade pattern with having few big customers, which could have a detrimental effect on the company's business results and balance sheet, together with the insurers' and his reinsurers' exposure to the same, the insured company is the most concerned with the insurance limits for its key buyers. On the other hand, this can be an important issue in negotiating with the insurer where not only the size of the exposures, but also their combination with the previous experience, creditworthiness, and financial strength of the buyers, do matter. Willingness and capabilities of the insurer to approve desired and adequate credit limits is usually—apart from insurance premium rates and other insurance conditions—one of the crucial elements of the insurer's competitive advantages. Speed of this service may be a matter of concern as well, particularly with regard to insurance limits and response of the credit insurer, especially online *via* e-commerce supported by accessible products and developed IT with large quantities of accurate data available and including automation of back-office processes. When applying for insurance limits or for their increase it is definitely worth asking and talking with the underwriters about their perception of risk and the company's needs and expectations. The parties of the credit insurance contract may not necessarily always agree with the views of each other. Credit insurers are specialist in credit insurance while the company knows and has better understanding of its business and thus can challenge their opinions. The company's specific information, purpose of the credit or of the goods supplied, business relations and dependence of the commercial partners, their ownership structure and market position as well as good previous experience with the buyer may help to justify a larger insurance limit and to encourage and persuade the underwriter.

It may be permitted for experienced companies with advanced credit risk management to set on the basis of accurate credit information the **discretionary insurance limits** for their known buyers with favorable payment experience independently, up to the Maximum Discretionary Limit, without prior approval of the insurer. But in claims handling procedure, the insured may have to justify on what basis it set these limits.

Therefore, for known buyers with good trading experience and without significantly late payments recorded where outstanding trade receivables represent smaller amounts, for example, EUR 15,000 or 25,000, "automatic limits' can be allocated. Such 'automatic limits' are often combined with the smaller insured percentage (higher insured's self-retention), for example, from normal 85 to 70 percent or 15 to 30 percent, respectively. For buyers with such insurance limits underwriting is simplified on a conveyer belt basis (negative vetting) and special credit information is not needed. Within these limits, that is, total amount of the buyer's outstanding debts, properly declared trade receivables are thus covered 'automatically'.

Some insurers even apply so called 'small automatic limits' with the simplified administration of the insurance policy; notifications of payment delays are not necessary, ascertainment of losses and claims handling are facilitated, etc.

The request for insurance limits can have **credit information** on buyers enclosed, if available, but it has to be up to date, for example, not more than 3 or 6 months old. More often in practice such information is provided by the insurer from his own or external sources.

If **credit reports** for certain buyers or buyers from certain countries are not available, the insurer may ask the insured to provide the latest balance sheets and other information available, for example, ownership structure, sales volume, number of employees, trading history, main suppliers, and buyers, etc. Such information will be most probably requested and obtained from the buyer himself. If not provided, or if such credit information proved to be unsatisfactory or does not suggest sound and stable position, the insurer may reject his approval, extension, or increase of the insurance limit and may appraise the insured of reduction or cancellation of insurance limits for his new business effective as of the date specified in the statement, though not earlier than the date of the receipt of notification.

Even for whole turnover insurance credit insurer is not obliged to insure all the risks, especially the worst risks and without additional collateral. Buyer's **creditworthiness** and his adequate credit rating is crucial for the insurer's decision whether to insure trade receivables for such buyer and to what extent or up to set credit (insurance) limit. It is no good and not wise to be exposed too much to debtors with not sufficient creditworthiness for deliveries on deferred payment terms.

Rejected or approved, even partially or conditionally approved, insurance limit is useful information for the insured companies to acknowledge which buyers are worth to trade with on deferred payment terms up to a certain amount on an open account basis. They can take the advantage of this information to set their sales policy as well as to change it according to the changes of insurance limits as a result of the insurer's risk monitoring. Risk monitoring may show the deterioration of the debtor's creditworthiness—which might require the cessation of deliveries on credit terms without advance payments and additional securities or to shorten the payment terms—or, on the other hand, its improvement. In the latter case, in order to increase sales to particular buyer, the insurance limit can be increased on request as in case of a temporary increase to cover seasonal supplies.

Dynamic management of the insurance limits enables credit insurers to exercise control over the exposure and their risk portfolio as well as their credit risk portfolio management with preventive and curative reactions to the problems which threaten or may threaten the debtors and trade receivables of the insured companies.

After the conclusion of the insurance contract **insurance cover becomes effective with the date stipulated in the written approval of the**

insurance limit, while the insurance actually begins upon delivery and with the submitted insurance declarations under the condition that due insurance premium is paid. The debtor's limits can be approved for 1 year, sometimes also conditionally, but in case of big risks they may be also set for a shorter duration. Insurance limits are checked from time to time and eventually altered by the insurer in its sole and absolute discretion at any given time. Whereas credit insurance premium rates are fixed for policy period and can be raised for new contracts only, dynamic insurance limit management is crucial for credit insurers and enables them to control their short-term credit risk exposures directly and to quickly react to deteriorating risks even before they become severe by lowering supply.

This degree of control to manage insurance limits also distinguishes credit insurance from other types of insurance as well as from other personal securities and financial instruments. Credit insurance cover for particular debtor is hence normally terminated with the lapse of the mentioned period of time, or canceled before time with the **notification of the insured on cancellation of the insurance limit.** With the aim to cut down the insurer's exposure and to prevent the companies to do business with unsound buyers such reduction or cancellation of credit insurance limits can apply, of course, only to shipments and deliveries made or dispatched after such notice is being received by the insured. On the other hand, apart from changes of insurance limits due to changes in risk underwritten these alterations may be provided by the needs of the insured and changes in his trade pattern. The insured usually apply for credit limit when it is needed for a new customer, to cover seasonal or increased supplies to existing one, when the insured foresee that the outstanding balance (payable and not yet due invoices) will exceed the existing limits, for coverage of one single delivery and for a transfer of credit limit in case of changed name, address, and legal status of a debtor.

Commencement of cover. Insurance contract covers credits (deliveries/ accounts receivable) during an insurance policy period which follows its conclusion or after its effective date and effective date of set insurance limits. Usually insurance contract becomes effective the first next day after its signing by the representatives of the both parties or the day when the insurer receives signed contract from the insured party. If so stipulated in the insurance contract, existing trade receivables—issued invoices or dispatches—prior to these dates may also be covered as long as they are still not due.

Insurance cover can be given on **risk attaching** or **loss occurring** basis. Legally valid trade receivables in the former case—where insurance premium is calculated on a declared turnover basis—are covered from the commencement of the risk and covered insured event can occur even outside the policy period. In the latter case of the loss occurring policy where the premium is calculated on the basis of the outstanding invoices, the insured event must occur during the policy period and it does not matter when the credit period started or the invoice was issued. That means, credits given before the effective date of the insurance policy may be insured, but on the other hand, after the termination of the insurance policy period outstanding trade receivables are no longer covered, except under renewed insurance policy.

4.2.4 Insurance Contract
4.2.4.1 Embracing Main Content
First draft of the insurance contract is usually prepared as a framework offer on the basis of the insured's initial request for insurance with the questionnaire. Final offer is then prepared on the basis of insurance limits requests and received and assessed credit information. This offer *(oferta)* comprises full set of insurance conditions for accepted credit risk portfolio of the insured for his eligible export and/or domestic business transactions on short-term credit terms up to the maximum credit period allowed covering commercial and/or noncommercial credit risk as well as PCR cover as its supplement, if needed, including insurance premium rates, etc. Figure 4.2 illustrates a more or less typical risk profile in manufacturing and credit risk period after delivery of the goods.

Underlying contracts. It is worth mentioning that the insurance conditions need to be adjusted to commercial terms and conditions, especially payment terms and conditions of the underlying contracts, and *vice versa*. Commercial contract provisions are also important for credit insurance. If the payment must be effected in 90 days after the dispatch, unpaid seller can expect this payment or claim payment from the insurer in accordance with the insurance conditions. On the other hand, if the payment terms are, for example, 60 days after the

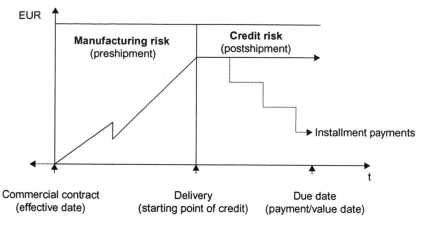

Figure 4.2 Risk profile (preshipment/postshipment).

acceptance of goods in the buyer's country, the payment is conditional upon the buyer's acceptance which can be out of control of the exporter, and there may be also some tricky questions about the delivery, transport insurance, export/import licenses and responsibilities of the parties of the underlying contract. Therefore, it may be crucial to have thoroughly prepared commercial contracts including binding settlement of disputes and governing law clauses and credit insurance policy should recognize applied contracting methodology as well as trade pattern and markets of the insured. It is equally important to have clear idea when the company wants the insurance cover for his buyers to commence as well as to end in order to avoid this to fall outside of the insurance policy terms either because the due date after its expiration or because of the credit period.

PCR. Unless the seller is not exposed to preshipment risk it is recommended to add appropriate PCR cover to ordinary credit insurance policy and thereby insures the company also against loss-causing events in the preshipment period. Unlike the credit risk period which is in insurance conditions conventionally expressed in days, PCR period is usually expressed in moths. PCR insurance cover commences on the effective date of the underlying commercial contract and typically extends until the forecasted final date of dispatch or invoice when the credit risk cover begins, in practice 6–12 months. If the stage payments are agreed for invoicing, the insured should have them covered with the postshipment insurance as they are invoiced. It is important for the insured company to have its business insured in such order to reflect and match the terms of its commercial contracts and insurance policy wording to ensure that there is no gap in preshipment and post-shipment cover, for example, the former should not be terminated before delivery, acceptance or invoicing and the commencement of the credit period. For preshipment insurance, it is better to have it on a risk attaching basis to cover the entire contract even the final dispatch comes after the insurance policy period. Furthermore, since credit insurers normally limit the maximum PCR period in the credit limit decisions, the insured should also advise him as soon as he has an indication or reason to expect the period for completion of his performance will be extended because of delays.

INSURED PORTFOLIO. As explained in describing the main features of credit insurance cover (see Section 3.1.5), standard short-term credit insurance policies attempt to avoid adverse selection of risks and cover eligible export and/or domestic trade credits with the pursuing the principles of **whole turnover insurance**—or also acceptable **spread insurance cover**—except transactions with the affiliated companies and business transactions where L/C or bank guarantees are issued, etc. In addition to prevailing whole turnover policies and their variants, that is, **multiple market** and **country turnover policies**, with **proportional insurance** coverage, in practice we can also find **specific account insurance policies** and wide range of **nonproportional insurances** for agreed selection of risks for big companies with sophisticated risk management. In practice, typical selection of risk to achieve insurance of acceptable spread of risk and to focus on main lines of business of the insured can include cover for markets in developed or developing countries only, can be limited to trade with certain goods, includes large exposures only, and can exclude longer credit risks, etc. Last but not least, some difficult markets and high-risk countries and the buyers from such countries may be generally off cover for private market insurers and sometimes even for national ECAs providing export credit insurance against political and other nonmarketable risks on behalf of their states or with their reinsurance or guarantees.

RISKS INSURED. Credit insurance policies are frequently combined and cover domestic and export trade of the companies on a global basis, and the latter cover is often comprehensive to provide insurance protection against both **commercial and political risks** in package. But there are generally several possibilities and combinations available. In most cases short-term credits for private buyers from politically stable and developed countries will be insured against commercial risk of insolvency and protracted default only, including the risks of the public buyers in such countries—which is otherwise perceived as a political risk, while political and other noncommercial risks for these buyers will be explicitly excluded from cover. On the other hand, credits to buyers in non-OECD countries, for example, will be insured against both commercial and noncommercial risks (with standard exclusions of certain risks in private market), as the latter are not trivial and may also lead to occurrence of commercial risks, nor nonexistent as, by definition, in case of domestic credits to private buyers.

4.2.4.2 Main Legal Characteristics

INSTEAD OF DEFINITION. With credit insurance contract the insured company insures agreed manufacturing and/or trade credit risk portfolio with the insurance company against commercial and/or noncommercial risks. For due insurance premium paid to credit insurer it receives efficacious financial protection for its valid trade receivables or unpaid outstanding debts of its buyers and the insurer's conditional personal guarantee *("policere")* to be, after the lapse of the waiting period, indemnified for any direct material loss sustained *(damnum emergens)*—less deductibles—with the effected claims payment if the risks underwritten from the underlying commercial contracts materialize due to loss-causing events and perils that according to applicable general and special insurance conditions, and so far these conditions are fulfilled, represent the insured event, that is, permanent insolvency or protracted default of the debtor, his guarantor, etc.

LEGAL NATURE. The company may accept the insurer's offer or may continue with negotiations to reach final agreement and to successfully conclude general credit **insurance contract**. Insurance contract is a special civil law institute and contract of indemnity by which the promisor agrees to reimburse a promisee for the loss irrespective of a third person's liability. With certain technical and legal specifics of credit insurance contract, this contract and its essential and other constituents and contract clauses *(essentialia* and *naturalia negotii)* are usually regulated as bilateral, onerous, compensatory, reciprocal and stand-alone contract with accessory and conditional monetary obligations of the insurer that holds the elements of an aleatory nature. Concluded typical credit insurance contract is a legal foundation of a long-term or permanent and intensive day-to-day cooperation in credit risk management between professional business partners, namely, credit insurance company and the insured party.

Legal base *(causa)* for credit insurance contract is in provided insurance cover for trade receivables of the insured and his related pecuniary interest *(securitas)* which is—in addition to auxiliary credit insurance services—the subject matter of the insurer's obligations, while the payment of insurance premium is main and reciprocal obligation of the insured party.

Credit insurance contract is a nominate, consensual and typically **long-term general agreement in writing** subject to annual and often automatic **renewals** (evergreen contract)—credit insurance policy is normally perpetual and is tacitly renewed for another policy period unless written notice of cancellation is given prior to its expiry—or permanent contract concluded for indefinite time period with the prescribed terms and conditions for its cancellation or termination, that is, formal termination of insurance with the same result as with the fulfillment of all contractual obligations of both parties ("natural expiry"). Even after the lapse of **insurance policy period**, insurance contract cancellation and termination, insurance cover for properly declared trade receivables with due insurance premium paid remains in force, for example, debtor's insolvency proceedings can be initiated even after the debts become due and after the lapse of the insurance policy period or its termination.

In certain sense credit insurance contract is a **framework contract** that *per se* does not provide full insurance coverage. Credit insurance cover becomes effective with and within the frame of set debtors' credit limits ("main contracts") and insurance conditions stipulated in these decisions and properly submitted insurance declaration. As already mentioned in Section 4.2.3, credit insurance contracts are **"revolving,"** subject to renewals and changes of insurance limits. They are written in **insurance policies** which represent documentary evidence of the conclusion of insurance contracts and their content with their essential constituents and clauses as well as with enclosed general and special conditions, requests for insurance, etc., as their integral parts.

Applicable Laws and General Insurance Conditions

Credit insurance contracts belong to insurance law in a broader sense that regulates contractual relationship between the parties of the insurance contract with special legal norms and nowadays becomes peculiar and relatively independent legal science as a part of civil material law on obligations or commercial law. Nevertheless, obligations stemming from credit insurance contracts are rather specific in underwriting as well as in legal sense. Therefore, credit insurance are regulated in more detail in legal norms of **autonomous business law**, that is, in model and **standard form insurance contracts** or in particular insurance contracts and attached general insurance conditions (*lex contractus*). But anyway, also for these contractual relationships various mandatory legal provisions (*ius cogens*) of governing laws as well as dispositive norms of commercial and civil laws (*ius dispositivum*)—in particular of their general parts—are applied, unless the use of the latter is excluded for credit insurance contracts due to their specifics.

Credit insurer concludes insurance contracts more or less of the same kind with a great and indefinite number of companies. It is therefore logical for the insurers to have prepared model forms and standard form insurance policies and their regular clauses. Such clauses may be also assembled in **general** or **special insurance conditions** that may be included in insurance contracts and enclosed to credit insurance policies as their integral parts.

All rights and obligations of credit insurance contract parties normally cannot be contained in insurance policy, despite this is also possible to certain extent and even common in practice of some insurers. In such case the text of the insurance policy would be more extensive and due to complexity of such insurance contract perhaps also less clear and understandable. But on the other hand, it may be better tailor-made and easier for negotiations. Under usual arrangements for credit insurance contracts, credit insurance policy comprises individual constituents while the full set of rights and obligations of the contract parties are embodied in wider text of general insurance conditions attached to the policy. The insured must get general insurance conditions, has to be acquainted with them when he enters into the contract and must explicitly agree to be an integral part of his insurance contract. Of course, any ambiguity or discrepancy in these documents should be avoided, but some particularities in special conditions which complement general insurance conditions may also be regulated differently in insurance policy and may deviate from general insurance conditions; in such case of a conflict, discrepancy, or inconsistency, the text of the insurance policy and its clauses shall take precedence over and derogate the provisions of general insurance conditions.

General credit insurance conditions prepared by the experts, approved by reinsurers and accepted by business practice are part of the offer of the credit insurer. Credit insurance contracts are more or less of a **standard form** with the **general** and perhaps particular **insurance conditions** and clauses attached. But that does not mean *per se*, that credit insurance contract amounts to **adhesion** or "boilerplate" **contracts**—that is, "take it or leave it" — that do not allow for negotiation, especially regarding their particular elements. Credit insurer will be most probably willing to withdraw from his more or less customary practice, if this is reasonable, depending on his market and negotiating position, available insurance capacities and appetite for risks, and may be willing to derogate from standard clauses to adjust his services to the needs of the insured parties.

Credit insurance involves important business relations and may have important and material repercussions on the contracting parties. Therefore, the insured needs to be well acquainted with insurance conditions. Unfair clauses that do not comply with good usages in business practice or are too rigorous regarding the circumstances are not allowed by general rules of laws on obligations and may be even null and void. Insurance conditions imposed and excessively unfair to the insured may held to be unenforceable because the consideration is lacking or is inadequate (unconscientious dealings), especially when the insurance contract is entered into between unequal bargaining parties and the insured party is not in a position to negotiate standard and fair insurance conditions.

In doubt and in case of unclear clauses the court of law will most probably interpret ("*Ius semper loquitur.*") insurance conditions contra proferentem, that is, in favor of a (weaker (?)) party who did not prepare or did not draft or propose (general) insurance conditions. Burden of any ambiguity and unclear clauses is by the ambiguity doctrine and old generally accepted civil law rule—"*in dubio contra stipulatorem*"—borne by the party who has caused the ambiguity, and among different interpretations the most favorable for the counterparty will be chosen. But it would be unwise to always count on that. Despite, and with the applied rules of the laws on obligations for other (property) insurance contracts by analogy, unclear clauses will be probably interpreted in favor of the insured party—which is when we talk about credit insurance usually commercial company (!)—and against the insurer, the companies do not need to rely on that entirely. It may also happen that general insurance conditions as an integral part of the insurance contract are not result of the insurer's superior bargaining power or knowledge and the insured's lack of choice, but the reflection of the autonomy of the contracting parties' will and that the parties explicitly agreed with these and such (customary (?)) conditions by the signing of the insurance contract. Due to sanctity of contracts concluded contracts are binding for the contracting parties—*pacta sunt servanda, but within the contents of the contracts and not beyond them.*

Although according to applicable laws, general insurance conditions should be known, clear and understandable for the insured as well as without any ambiguity, some clauses may sometimes leave a room open for their interpretation. Such "approach" is to a certain extent understandable due to the nature of general legal norms and various actual circumstances on the other hand. Credit insurers, perhaps much more than other (composite) insurance companies, are usually more inclined to satisfy the expectations of the insured parties to find the solutions for their problems as well as in claims handling procedures. Nevertheless, credit insurer and the insured company are long-term business partners in risk management. Therefore, credit insurers might be flexible in interpreting their insurance conditions, but only when the behavior of the insured, circumstances and the insured event allow so.

MAIN ELEMENTS OF CREDIT INSURANCE CONTRACTS. Insurance contracts as well as insurers' offers usually comprise similar constituents, such as preamble with specified firms of the contracting parties and their coordinates, representations and warranties, provisions on effectiveness and duration of insurance contract and insurance cover periods, various contract terms, etc. Moreover, detailed insurance conditions for each and every buyer, accepted for cover up to insurance limits—eventually also set for their countries—are also stipulated in credit insurance contracts, including *inter alia*:

- description of insurance cover for eligible short-term commercial transactions or trade receivables, that is, subject matter of credit insurance with the maximum credit periods, against manufacturing and/or credit commercial and/or noncommercial risks (specified insured events) within set insurance limits, which are constituent element of the insurance contract, with insurance conditions and accompanied with the exclusions and limitations of the insurer's liability;
- insured percentage or self-retention of the insured and other deductibles;
- maturity of the insurer's obligations to pay claims and methods of their fulfillment;
- insurance premium rates that reflects the risks underwritten and ceded risk portfolio;
- provisions when the premium comes due and the manner, method and place of payments;

- assignment of insurance policy rights and subrogation;
- notices, administration of credit insurance policy, debt collection, claims handling, and recoveries;
- detailed obligations and duties of the insured in the policy period and sanctions for infringements;
- confidentiality of credit insurance contract and underlying commercial contracts;
- applicable laws and settlement of disputes;
- miscellaneous and final provisions.

Commercial and insurance practice is rapidly and constantly changing, old—fashioned credit insurance services are now giving way also to new and different form of credit insurance contracts, and general insurance conditions are constantly evolving. It has to be mentioned that the trends toward serviced credit insurance leads to more and more **combined** credit insurance **contracts** with the characteristics of **mixed service contracts** and prevailing more or less typical clauses for insurance contracts as well as clauses of other contracts and legal provisions for particular contracts of civil and commercial laws.

With the conclusion of the insurance contract credit insurer and the insured company enter into long-term insurance relationship and here we usually talk about formal commencement of the insurance. In theory we also talk about material or actual commencement of insurance when insurance coverage commences for insured credits given to particular buyers as stipulated in insurance contract and/or its general and special insurance conditions enclosed as well as with the effective date of set insurance limits; this insurance period can start with the inception date or certain event. But on the other hand, we can also talk about actual material commencement of insurance cover which is linked to obligations of the insured to submit insurance declarations and is valid upon the condition that due insurance premium is paid. Furthermore, we can also talk about technical commencement of the insurance relationship which commences with the date from which the insurer calculates insurance premiums.

4.2.4.3 Insurance Limits
Properly declared short-term trade receivables—usually expressed in monetary value of the invoices with the VAT excluded or included and without default interest, liquidated damages and penalties—are

covered with the insurance contract up to the **insurance limits** set for the buyers (debtors). The setting of insurance limits is of paramount importance for credit insurers to control, to measure and to mitigate the risks underwritten.

These approved credit limits of outstanding debts represent the "sum insured" or upper amount of claims paid in accordance with insurance conditions as an indemnity for direct material loss incurred due to occurrence of the insured event and reduced by the self-retention of the insured. These insurance limits comprise accumulated outstanding debts of the buyers (balance) and are set on **revolving** basis. From this point of view credit insurance may be similar to floating insurance policies as the "sum insured" or value of the subject matter of credit insurance is floating, for example, balance of outstanding debts are changing in the policy period similarly to value of goods in stock in fire insurance.

Such system for establishing and limiting the amount of credit insurer's liability is logical and righteous because it prevents claims paid in indemnity insurance to exceed the loss sustained *(damnum emergens)* and unjust enrichment of the insured party. This is an outcome of applied principle of indemnity—credit insurance as well as suretyship and liability insurance belong to indemnity insurance—where the insurer compensates the insured for material loss incurred without the lost profit *(lucrum cessans)*, etc.

To set adequate insurance limits in addition to assessment of creditworthiness of the buyers it is important for the insured to acquaint the insurer with his existing and forecasted trade volume, dynamics of deliveries and payment terms, that is, flow charts or credit risk exposure profile including PCR and sufficient contingency for eventual delays for shipments and payments. On the basis of these data from **insurance limit request** (credit limit application form) as well as considering tolerated late payments—which are also indicated in the **list of approved credit limits**—insurance limits will be set; sometimes also conditionally, for example, that the insured has to submit the freshest balance sheet or (favorable) credit report or trade references for his buyer for any continuance, renewal, extension, or increase of approved insurance limit. It is very important for the insured to ensure the requested credit limits are sufficient to cover all deliveries and outstanding trade receivables including their overlaps at one time.

For stable turnover the insured's application for credit insurance limit of a particular buyer may be, for instance, based on the following simple formula:

$$L = t(c + 1)$$

where

L = insurance (credit) limit;
t = envisaged annual turnover divided by 12;
c = credit period (expressed in months).

For temporary peaks the insured may use the same formula and then apply for temporary increases to cover seasonal peaks, or may apply for insurance limit, for example, by taking into account his estimated monthly maximum turnover.

Example:
• For annual sales turnover of EUR 1.2 million with successive and equal deliveries (stable monthly turnover) in the amount of EUR 100,000 per month, payment terms of 60 days and tolerated late payments of 35 days, for example, "optimal" adequate insurance limit can be set in the amount of EUR 400,000.

This example is also illustrated in Figure 4.3.

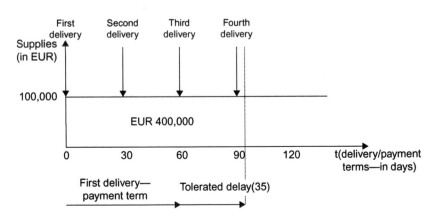

Figure 4.3 Sales and buyer's insurance limit.

As already said, these insurance (credit) limits are "filled up" or "emptied" with the effectiveness of accounts receivable or paid debts. Outstanding invoices are covered on **revolving** basis in their chronological order up to the amount of the operative insurance limits set for all business of the insured, or temporary increased for seasonal or extraordinary approved deliveries. Approved and valid insurance limit represents maximum amount of accumulated covered outstanding debts (invoices) of a particular buyer up to which the insured is entitled to submit his request for claims payment. That means, the outstanding debts in excess of set insurance limits (overloading) are not covered and these residual risks and losses have to be borne by the insured. This is better not to be neglected in practice because **overloading** proved not to be rare when the insurers check circumstances in their claims handling. For overtrading which may increase payment default risk the insured's request for claim payment can be even rejected. The insurer may also demand from the insured to proportionally reduce his request for claims payment for all payments effected by his debtor for uninsured outstanding debts in excess of set credit limit.

Actual material loss without consequential losses and compensation for lost profit, that is, principal amount and regular interest *(sortem et usuras)*, if the latter are agreed for short-term credits and are explicitly covered, incurred to the insured due to insolvency of his buyer or protracted default—while default interest accrued after the due date for payment and penalties are usually not covered—will be compensated up to the set insurance limit. For these unpaid and overdue outstanding debts within the operative credit limits the insured will be indemnified in proportion to the agreed **insured percentage**, that is, the amount of loss incurred for the claim payment will be additionally reduced by insured's self-retention or any other deductible.

Proportional short-term credit insurance against commercial risks has more or less standard **self-retention** rate of 15 percent and its reciprocal value, that is, insured percentage, 85 percent. Percentage of cover may also be lower, for example, even 50 percent for risky business deals where this requires different risk sharing between the partners, or for insurance in high-risk markets, but may be also higher, for example, 90, 95, and even 100 percent, for medium-term export credits, PRI, or because of the needs of the insured.

Example:

- For overdue outstanding debts in the amount of EUR 100,000 where the insurance limit is set for EUR 200,000 and after the institution of the buyer's bankruptcy the insured shall file the request for claims payment in the amount of EUR 100,000. With the agreed insured's self-retention of 10 percent the insurer shall indemnify him for the loss incurred according to insured percentage of 90 percent with the claim payment in the amount of EUR 90,000 while the insured shall borne his remaining self-retention in the amount of EUR 10,000.

TERMINATION OF INSURANCE CONTRACT AND MODIFICATION OF INSURANCE CONDITIONS. Credit insurance contracts are usually permanent contracts with prescribed rules for their termination or cancellation and are normally subject to (automatic) annual renewals (evergreen contracts). Insurance cover may also vary during the policy period in accordance with changes in risks underwritten, trade pattern of the insured or his volume of trade as well as with accordingly altered credit risk portfolio insured, for example, set insurance limits may at any time alter, decrease or increase, old buyers' credit limits may be extended, canceled or changed as well as new insurance limits for new buyers may be set, and furthermore, insurance cover may be extended to new buyers from other countries, insurance cover can be withdrawn for buyers in certain countries and cover for new risks can be added to the existing, extended or new insurance policy (PCR and/or noncommercial risks insurance, etc.), insurance premium rates and various other insurance conditions, for example, self-retention of the insured, may also be changed or modified for new credits and policy periods, etc. It is normally allowed for credit insurer also to modify or amend his general and special insurance conditions with prior written notice and receipt theory applied, but the insured then has an option to terminate insurance contract. If the contract does not cease to be valid trade receivables declared after the notice is received are insured under new conditions. The insurer is usually explicitly obliged to inform also the assignee about any changes in the insurance conditions made after the assignment of insurance policy rights.

General insurance conditions may also specifically prescribe that insurance contract is terminated with immediate effect when the insured becomes insolvent or is the subject of insolvency proceedings as well as with the cessation of his business activities.

4.3 CREDIT INSURANCE POLICY ADMINISTRATION

4.3.1 General

Credit insurance is a rather complex and difficult type of insurance for the insured company that demands active involvement of its staff and requires proper decisions on strategic and management level, division of labor and responsibilities as well as coordination of day-to-day activities. When credit insurance is a novelty for the company's business and its credit risk management, the company has to establish appropriate organizational structure for its business activities, sales, finances, accounting and risk management including developed IS, reporting and control with well–qualified and properly trained employees. By bearing in mind complexity, administrative burden and more demanding working process in the credit insured company— usually much more than most other insurances require—this may well illustrate the way in which credit insurance has an impact on the whole business of the company and affects many areas. Therefore, credit insurance also always requires an involvement at high management level. After all, with the concluded whole turnover credit insurance contract profound changes may quite disturb ordinary and traditional approach, existent behavior and processes of various organizational units, for example, commercial department, shipping department, financial or accounting offices, legal department, treasury, etc.

There is no magic recipe what is the most appropriate **organizational structure** for activities associated with credit insurance in the company and where should certain responsibilities sit. For certain companies it would be appropriate to have these attached to sales department, for others finance department or special risk management unit or treasury would be more appropriate solution. Nevertheless, at the end it depends mostly on each particular company and its size, but each decision must take into account credit insurance policy administration and operation, certain procedures and the duties of the insured to comply with insurance terms and conditions. In this respect, experience and advice of the underwriter or insurance broker can be helpful.

At first glance, all these activities and sophisticated credit insurance procedures sound like big burden for the credit insured company, but it is unavoidable and useful contribution for good **credit risk management** of the company that save costs. By virtue of outsourcing, taking out credit insurance and complying with the insurance conditions and requirements, for example, credit risk assessment is ensured, credit limits and maximum credit term periods for buyers are set, risk monitoring is performed, credit risk exposure is controlled, overdue accounts receivable are highlighted, debt collection can be more efficient, etc. On the other hand, these procedures and requirements can also be used to achieve synergies and to impose good governance and common practice across existing companies in the group as well as for new acquisitions.

INFORMATION SYSTEM. In addition to organizational measures developed computerized IS for credit control is very important also for operating credit insurance policies. It is useful to integrate credit risk assessment and credit limits setting with the acceptance of orders, shipments, invoicing and payments including credit terms and due dates. All these must be *inter alia* recorded, monitored and reviewed. If due payments are not effected, further business should be halted, insurer should be notified and debt collection activities should start.

It is worth not forgetting that the transfer of credit risks to the insurance company can definitely improve and facilitate credit risk management but can never replace it completely! Last but not least, it may decrease costs and time spent.

●●●──

Credit insurance is more like business partnership in risk management than financial product providing risk protection for the losses incurred with the claims paid.

───

With the signing of credit insurance contract the relations between the insurer and insured company are far from being finished. This is more the case with other insurances, excluding handling of claims and claims payment after the occurrence of the insured events. In credit insurance relations between the partners actually commence after the conclusion of the insurance contract. With the effectiveness of credit insurance cover these trust-based and long-term relations have an important impact on business results of both partners (follow the fortune).

Relations and contacts between the insurer and credit insured company intensify after the conclusion of the insurance contract. Business, risks, risk management, and activities to operate a credit insurance policy roll by and are continuing lively. This requires day-to-day and close-knitted relations and cooperation between partners, for example, insurance declarations must be submitted and due premium paid, late payments and changed circumstances have to be reported, requests for claims payments have to be submitted on time, the insured has to cooperate with the insurer in debt collections and recoveries, etc.

DUTIES OF THE INSURED. Because of information asymmetry in favor of credit insured company **the insured is obliged to act in good faith as if uninsured and professional expert with a higher standard of due diligence required.** In mutual interest of both long-term contracting parties, the insured must *inter alia* promptly and properly **inform the insurer about all relevant and material facts and circumstances related to his buyers and changes in trading environment that might influence the risks** underwritten, especially their deterioration. Moreover, the insured has to regularly and promptly report all unusual events and excessive payment delays which may lead to payment defaults and must **carry out all reasonable and necessary measures to prevent loss-causing events and to minimize losses,** including debt collection and recoveries. We can expect from the companies to be professional, to have efficient credit control over their accounts receivable and debtors, to control their orders, deliveries and outstanding debts of their buyers as well as to monitor their payments at due dates. Furthermore, we can also expect from the insured companies to regularly communicate with their buyers, to perform invoicing and debt collection activities, to institute and actively take part in legal procedures, if needed, etc.

4.3.2 Insurance Declarations and Premiums

Among the most important credit insurance conditions and fundamental obligations of the insured to be entitled to claims payment, crucial also for the existence of the insurance contract and coverage, is regular and prompt submission of duly completed **insurance declarations.** The insured has to declare—normally on monthly or quarterly basis for the previous period—and submit his statement with the list of all (new)

outstanding debts of his buyers with the set insurance limits in respect of all goods dispatched and/or services invoiced, that is, on the basis of agreed **turnover** or **balance declaring**. Among these trade receivables, fully or partly already paid debts, for example, *sconto cassa*, have to be declared as well, including those above the insurance limits. On the other hand, advance payments before deliveries and commercial transactions covered by bank instruments usually do not need to be declared.

DUTIES TO REPORT. Properly submitted complete insurance declarations are essential or **fundamental obligations of the insured** and failure to do this is stringent condition for validity and effectiveness of credit insurance cover. These declarations are used by the insurers to measure and analyze their risk exposure to individual debtors and guarantors, industry branches and countries as well as for purpose to collect insurance premium. On the basis of insurance declaration and insurance contract the insurance premium owed will be calculated and invoiced up to the amount of the whole declared insured turnover and notwithstanding eventual excess of trade over insurance limits approved for particular buyers; in fact, invoices for previous deliveries may be paid later on and insurance limits will be thus freed again also for these trade receivables, that is, tail-end risks. As already mentioned in Section 3.1.6, some credit insurers still apply balance declaring or so called open balance policies or may even calculate insurance premiums or special charges according to set insurance limits. Paid credit insurance premium is therefore usually dispersed over the insurance period according to actual trade volume and its dynamics.

INSURANCE PREMIUMS. As in other insurances, specific account credit insurance policies usually require that the insurance premium is paid up front in its entire amount after the conclusion of the insurance contract. This "anticipatory principle" may be applied sometimes also for whole turnover insurance or spread cover. In this case **deposit insurance premium** may be required as well and it is usually paid up front quarterly for the insured turnover during the previous period, while some credit insurers may also invoice and collect **minimum and deposit premium**. None of these is by the rule and as customary elsewhere in insurance industry, returnable or repayable.

For valid and effective insurance coverage and to be entitled to claims payment, in addition to properly reported insurance declaration of outstanding invoices due **payment of insurance premium** and other charges at the times specified **is a condition precedent for claims payment**. **Underdeclaration** or failure to comply with insurance conditions and to pay due insurance premiums (lapsed insurance policy) on all business insured are usually sufficient reasons for the insurer to charge additional premium for the time period in which the insured did not declare given credits. He is also entitled to reject the insured's request for claims payment for insured event occurred in the period for which the premium was not paid as well as to terminate the insurance contract from the date of notice and in accordance with insurance conditions. In the event of a breach of this condition precedent, the insurer normally also retains the right to already paid premiums and other charges. Underdeclaration is quite often a problem for credit insurers and may be discovered when the insurer makes a spot checking in accordance with insurance conditions that allow him to **inspect and audit records, books and documents of the insured**, or when the insured files the claim. In addition to mentioned contractual sanctions for the insured's infringements of insurance conditions, the insurer is usually also entitled to other customary sanctions and rights on the basis of general rules of commercial contract laws, that is, the right to demand execution of the contract, default interest, right of setoff, etc.

Transfer of insurance policy's rights. Insurance cover and claims payment are conditional upon the fulfillment of the insured's obligations. Therefore, when credit insurance is concluded on someone else's account, the loss payee (the assignee of the insurance policy rights, i.e., the bank) has to be very careful. Failure to submit insurance declarations for insured trade credits makes these transactions effectively uncovered and the claims paid for underdeclared accounts receivable may also be proportionally reduced for other credits. Infringements of the insured's duties definitely increase the risk of the beneficiary of the insurance policy not to get claims paid. With the **assignment of insurance policy rights** the insured party is not released from his liabilities and the insurer always retains against the assignee all the objections he may or might have against the insured (the assignor).

Insurance premium—including insurance premium tax, if prescribed—is usually paid by the insured, but it may be also paid by anyone with the legitimate interest, for example, the bank as the assignee, except by the buyer (the debtor) who does not have or should not have such interest. Even if such interest exists, this would have been evidently against the discreet nature of credit insurance and could have shown signs of moral hazard.

Currencies, places, and methods of payments, including foreign currency and interest rate clauses—within contractual freedom limited by mandatory rules of applicable monetary laws, foreign exchange regulations and civil or commercial laws, are stipulated in insurance contracts or general insurance conditions. The insurer is normally not obliged to warn and remind the insured of the payment of insurance premium and such exclusion is often explicitly stipulated in insurance conditions.

4.3.3 Exchange of Information and Insurance Limits

CHANGED RISK. Among other obligations of the insured company is to continuously inform the insurer about all facts and circumstances of which he is aware or should be aware of that may influence the risks underwritten and the ability of its debtors to settle their debts. According to the principle of good faith, provisions of insurance contract, general insurance conditions and as the risk is an essential element of credit insurance contract, the insured must report to the insurer also all adverse and changed circumstances. If needed, such information can be requested from the insured company on demand; otherwise, its insurance policy rights may be changed or even canceled.

Nevertheless, the exchange of information in credit insurance goes in both directions. The insured party is usually also entitled to receive credit information from its insurer who carries out permanent risk monitoring. Thus the insured company can continually adjust its sales and crediting policy toward its customers, as appropriate.

INSURANCE LIMITS. With the aim to actively manage the risk exposure and as already said in Sections 4.2.3 and 4.2.4, set insurance limits may be subject to *ex ante* alterations. The list of approved buyers' credit limits which is integral part of the insurance contract is changing from time to time in the policy period.

For instance, in whole turnover insurance policies or general insurance conditions it is usually prescribed that the insured company is obliged to offer the insurer to insure all of his eligible new customers and fill out for them appropriate **credit limit requests** including such requests for increase of set limits in case of envisaged increase of turn-over or outstanding covered debts. Set **insurance limits may alter** at any time and for any reason whatsoever by sent notice in writing, for example, increase or decrease in the policy period to reflect changes in credit and/or country risks underwritten or in trade pattern, and may be even canceled for subsequent deliveries while previous and existing trade receivables remain insured under old and unchanged conditions. Insurance limits can be regularly or exceptionally extended or changed for new credits, for example, regarding their amounts, payment terms, requested additional securities and other conditions. Moreover, new buyers with set insurance limits can be added to insurance contract, coverage can be withdrawn or extended to new countries, buyers from some countries can be excluded from insurance or may be insured under different conditions, requirements for ROT and other collateral can be eased or canceled, etc.

Credit limits management. Sales, financial, accounting, and other departments of the insured companies should regularly perform and monitor trade and financial flows with all buyers, exhaustion or avail-ability of set credit insurance limits as well as invoicing, outstanding trade receivables, and debt collection. In relation to the debtor, coordi-nation and cooperation of various internal departments, external consultants and different services providers is useful and often neces-sary. On the other hand, it is useful to keep the insurer up to date with the developments to ensure that the insurance coverage match the insured's trade pattern and needs, especially before the renewals of the insurance policy.

4.3.4 Notice of Late Payments and Discontinuing the Deliveries

OVERLOADING PROHIBITED. When the volume of trade on short-term credit with a particular buyer reaches set insurance limit, unless the limit is meanwhile extended on the request of the insured, or when the buyer does not pay his overdue debts according to contrac-tual credit terms increased for the handling time of the bank and when these late payments exceed tolerated usual delays specified in insurance contract or in enclosed list of insurance limits, and if the debtor is not in a position to settle his debts, for example, due to his illiquidity or insolvency, **the insured has to immediately halt further deliveries** unless otherwise is agreed with the insurer.

PREVENTION AND LOSS MINIMIZATION MEASURES. The demand to discontinue the deliveries is very important prohibition and obligation of the insured seller which prevent him to increase his credit risk exposure to such unreliable buyer imprudently. Payment delays also require from the insured to notify the insurer, to follow his instructions and to launch all reasonable debt collection activities and other countermeasures. When the insurance limits is filled up with overdue and unpaid debts this may be a serious sign of worsening debtor's liquidity or solvency. In such situation the creditor should behave and act as a **prudent professional**. He has to act at all times with due diligence and has to perform debt collection with due care, and **as if uninsured**, by using all reasonable efforts to prevent the occurrence of loss-causing event, to avoid or minimize the loss sustained, for example, he has to send invoices, to draw the debtor's attention and to remind him on (non)payments, to protest unhonored bills of exchange, to activate given securities, to attach, seize or secure the debtor's assets in his possession, etc. Even after the claim payment the insured must not do anything that could lessen or impair his or the insurer's rights in relation to the goods, debtors and guarantors.

Notifications. The insured has to report the insurer the buyer's commercial reclamations and intentions or proposals to return delivered goods, requested extensions of payment terms (the insured may not agree to any extension of due dates for payments and especially may not allow credit to run beyond specified maximum extension period), approved discounts, credit notes, or write-offs of the debts. Only if explanations for these are founded, notified and approved by the insurer, the insurance coverage for these parts of payments remains in force and is not lost for the insured. If, for example, the insurer agrees with the extension of payment period he would normally require that the negotiable instrument, if any, is replaced by one which is the same, except that it incorporates the extended due date. Likewise, the insured may not wholly or partially waive any right against the debtor without the consent of the insurer, nor may renounce from real and personal securities. If such failure has increased the loss, claim paid is adjusted.

Nevertheless, the insurer may allow and approve further sales to the buyer despite nonpayments if the insured's explanation and reasons are founded and reasonable. Continuing delivery of goods or performance of services might be necessary for the debtor to continue with the production and sales to earn financial means to repay his debts. For subsequent deliveries more stringent payment terms and conditions may be required and agreed between contracting parties including demands for additional securities, for such deliveries down-payments can be requested and part of them can be dedicated for decrease of the amount of outstanding debts, etc. Without specific approval of the insurer for such continued trade flows, subsequent deliveries when the buyer does not pay his overdue debts even in the time period of tolerated delays, as well the credits in excess of set insurance limits, are not covered, and the claims paid can be reduced while overloading that increases nonpayment risk may even lead to rejection of claims payment.

REPORTS ON PAYMENT DELAYS. Further to basic obligations of the insured company to properly submit insurance declarations and to pay insurance premiums due, for claims payment also the timely **notifications of payment delays** (overdue accounts declarations) are essential conditions precedent. This is not only valid for the first overdue covered debt but also for subsequent trade receivables to the buyer who has already been late with his payments. As said about the notice of late payments, the same obligation to report is also *mutatis mutandis* related to the buyers' proposals for partial payments, threats with forced compositions, bankruptcies, etc.

LEGAL CONSEQUENCES. When the payment terms are agreed or prescribed and unless agreed otherwise, payment delay commences after the due date, but normally the creditor has to remind the debtor to pay. Buyer's payment default may activate various legal or financial means of protection, for example, retention rights *(ius retentionis)*, liens and pledges, bank guarantees and similar undertakings, or may entitle unpaid creditors for contractual sanctions, penalties, etc. Nevertheless, delayed payments may also lead to general legal repercussions which can harden creditors' contractual rights and protect them against payment defaults of their counterparties, for example:

— possibility for additional request of the seller against the debtor to fulfill his obligations;
— transfer of risks;
— default interest;

— indemnity claims if the debtor can be blamed for default and unless explicitly agreed otherwise;
— various creditor's objections due to debtor's nonperformance, endangerment, etc.

All these means are usually available also for credit insured seller and/or insurer subrogated in his rights and are important for debt collection and recoveries.

DUTY TO NOTIFY. Notifications of payment defaults or payment delays—they represent **pending claims** for the insurer—must be complete and submitted on time in accordance with the insurance conditions. This is necessary for the insurer to adopt required measures and act properly to prevent occurrence of the insured event and minimize losses. Such notifications are required from the insured on the basis of applied insurance conditions, and for these obligations of the insured also the sanctions are prescribed. Some insurers do not require to notify every and each delay immediately, but only those exceeding *usual delays in payments*, or only those debts of the buyers whose the oldest overdue outstanding debts are longer than certain period of time, for example, 90 days.

Notifications of payment delays are usually submitted in special form with the following columns and content:

— reference number and date;
— amount, currency, and due date of the invoice or the list of outstanding debts due and not yet due of a particular buyer;
— description of given securities, if any;
— reasons for nonpayment, if known or assumed; and
— description of already executed, intended or suggested measures, and activities for debt collection.

According to insurance conditions, the insured is obliged to notify the insurer about payment default of the buyer immediately, but not later than 45, 60, 90, or 150 days after the due date for unpaid trade receivables and eventually given additional time period for tolerated delays, sometimes together with the list of another outstanding debts not yet due.

WAITING PERIOD. With the aim to avoid premature claims payment when the payments under underlying commercial contracts are only temporarily delayed and to allow the insurer enough time to examine all relevant circumstances, credit insurance conditions normally specify a CWP, that is, the earliest date after filing on which the claim can be paid and which usually vary from insurer to insurer and is different for different insured events. While for insolvencies the claims are paid more or less immediately, that is, in 15 or 30 days from the date of ascertainment of loss immediately after the occurrence of the debtor's insolvency, the claims for protracted default is usually payable in 6 months period, but this time period sometimes may be prolonged for riskier markets. Such waiting periods may have negative impact on the cash flow of the insured, but in case of a higher certainty about claims payment this payment might be recorded in the accounts of the insured as a trade receivable (short-term assets).

4.3.5 Debt Collection and Loss Minimization Measures

With agreed and reasonable measures to prevent loss-causing events, minimize losses and improve possibilities for their recoveries, the insured is obliged by insurance conditions—within his **duty to mitigate**—to carry out whatever is possible and reasonable and to cooperate with the insurer in debt collection. When the situation requires and it is a matter of urgency, the insured is allowed to act independently as a prudent trader but has to notify the insurer about his acts and measures without delay.

Among these measures including **cessation of further deliveries** for buyers with overdue outstanding debts and seizure of his assets one can also reckon, *inter alia*, repeated warning, **reminding** and personal visits to the debtor, debt restructuring and counterpurchasing. The seller involved with the buyer in long-term business relations, especially if the buyer is heavily dependent on the creditor, has better possibility to be paid and collect debts. Debt collection tactics and activities can be advised and recommended by the insurer, but this can also be a part of the credit insurer's auxiliary services provided by insurance company or its associated or other companies, for example, within serviced credit insurance.

DEBT COLLECTION. In their debt collection activities the companies may take part in **execution procedures** which is usually not easy under foreign jurisdictions and may cost dear, can be time consuming and might even be ill-advised because the debtor perhaps does not exist anymore or has no assets on disposal. The insured companies may be advised and assisted in their debt collections activities by the insurers' legal and claims departments, debt collection agencies and lawyers who are acquainted with local legislation, customs and legal procedures. Furthermore, global credit insurers may be supported in debt collection in foreign markets by their branches, subsidiaries and their local partners, ECAs can count on assistance of other national ECAs, other financial institutions, and diplomats, etc.

Expenses for debt collection services differ from one service provider to another and may be based on their tariffs and/or can be payable on success-fee basis. The prices usually depend on outstanding amounts, their age, and the country of the debtor. Debt collection agencies, for example, may charge certain amount already for the opening of the case, or can be paid on success-fee basis. They usually prefer and more often use out-of-court debt collection procedures and personal contacts with the debtors while the lawyers are more frequently used in case of commercial disputes.

It is well known that the success of debt collection activities depends heavily on immediate and appropriate steps and actions taken. Coordinated, consistent, and professional measures to minimize losses and debt collection—in practice majority of them are carried out extra judicially—are proven to be much more successful if started early after the due dates, and sometimes even earlier.

If and when in debt collection the credit insurer is directly or indirectly involved, the insurer would take account on applicable legislation in force and would pay attention to the interest of the insured and his business relationship with the buyer. The measures will be taken with the consent of the insured. If required, credit insurer—who is not dependent on the buyer as the insured and the buyer may also owe to other insured companies—shall contact the debtor personally, or shall use his local partners. Outsourcing of debt collection to specialized institution, that is, credit insurance company with know-how, professional experience and other capacities as well as links with financial institutions and other companies, is usually cost-effective and can be extremely useful. Its involvement may diminish **legal risks** as well as language barriers, and last but not least, this can also be *a good reason* for the debtor to settle his debts.

LIABILITY OF THE INSURED. To carry out all necessary and reasonable loss-causing event prevention and loss minimization measures is an essential obligation of the insured stipulated in insurance conditions. Infringement of these provisions, deliberate or negligent failure to act as a prudent seller may lead to rejection of his requests for claims payment or its reduction due to so incurred or increased loss. The insured can also terminate the insurance contract with the insured party who does not fulfill his obligations and does not carry out required and customary expected risk mitigation activities.

COVERED COSTS. Credit insurance does not have its active (*restitution*) function only, as mentioned in Section 2.2.2, that is, **financial indemnification** for the loss incurred because of the payment default of the buyer. Auxiliary functions of credit insurance are also **prevention and curative functions** related to prevention of loss-causing events and their consequences with the minimization of losses sustained and recovered claims paid. Therefore, similarly to various other property insurances not only claims paid for loss incurred are the result of credit insurance cover. Credit insurers also cover salvage and similar costs of the insured spent for loss prevention and minimization activities. The liability of credit insurer may therefore even increase *the sum insured*, that is, insured percentage of unpaid covered trade receivables. In addition to claims paid **credit insurers reimburse the insured parties also for their expenses for debt collection, execution and insolvency proceedings**, etc. Upon the occurrence of the insured event as stipulated in insurance conditions and in addition to claims paid up to the insurance limits, the insurer partly indemnifies the insured also for his costs related to loss prevention and minimization activities. These expenses covered by the insurer are generally shared between the contracting parties according to agreed percentage of insurance coverage. However, this reimbursement is anyway limited to external or additional and reasonable costs for agreed and founded loss prevention and minimization measures. Moreover, from the insured it is normally required to get the **approval of the insurer** prior to these activities, except in case of urgency. Nevertheless, *ex post* consent of the insurer is not needed for taxes and other charges in bankruptcy proceedings because the filing of petition in insolvency proceedings is the explicit obligation of the insured. It needs to be mentioned for the conclusion that all these costs are covered notwithstanding the success or failure of the measures taken.

These covered costs include required, reasonable and documented *external* direct costs for debt collection, while indirect costs, such as costs of bridge financing, administration costs and usual, *own* or internal additional costs of the insured related to, for example, substantiating the claim, settling technical and commercial disputes and reminding of the debtors are not covered. Costs for prevention and loss minimization activities of the companies—especially during the stages of *normal business relations* with the buyer when the risk of occurrence of the insured event is still hypothetical or an abstract one—credit insurers do not cover but may be borne by the debtor according to underlying commercial contract. Neither when the covered risk is materializing and is becoming real and not only hypothetical one, for example, payment delays or other events characteristical for the buyer's insolvency, credit insurer does not cover mentioned *own costs* of the insured with debt collection activities. The insured company must manage its risks including debt collection prudently anyway and like its trade receivables are not insured. On the other hand, the insurers do not invoice their *own* expenses for risk management, debt collection and recoveries neither, except when these services are provided separately or within serviced credit insurance.

Example:
- Insured event—buyer's bankruptcy: set insurance limit—EUR 100,000, insured's self-retention—15 percent, overdue debts (nonpaid invoices)—EUR 80,000, *external* costs for debt collection of the insured—EUR 10,000 and his *own* internal costs—EUR 3,000.

	Credit insurer reimburses
(i) claim paid	EUR 68,000 (EUR 80,000−12,000 (i.e., 15 percent))
(ii) costs	EUR 8,500 (EUR 10,000–1,500 (i.e., 15 percent))
	Total EUR 76,500

4.4 CLAIMS HANDLING

4.4.1 Request for Claims Payment

Credit insurer should be informed about all important facts and circumstances as well as the occurrence of the insured event must be reported to him as required by the insurance conditions. On the basis of this information credit insurer can make an estimation regarding the loss and its amount as well as the liability to indemnify the insured with the claim payment.

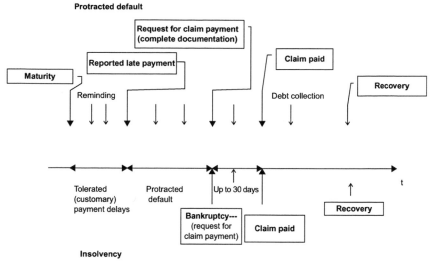

Figure 4.4 Claims handling.

DUTY TO NOTIFY THE INSURER. Covered loss-causing event is usually under the control or at least in the sphere of the insured and his business relations. Therefore, complete and timely submitted **notification of the insured about the occurrence of the insured event** and the loss incurred is a logical condition precedent for fulfillment of the insurer's obligation to pay claim. On the other hand, this duty of notification is also important for successful later recoveries of the claims paid from the debtor or his guarantors. This notification is the first phase and required activity in the claims handling procedure as described in this section and also displayed in Figure 4.4.

In agreed period of time after the occurrence of the insured event— when certain loss-causing event occurs is stipulated in insurance conditions—the insured must in addition to already submitted notification of payment delay file the **request for claims payment with complete set of requested documents evidencing the occurrence of the insured event and the amount of loss incurred.**

Duty to notify the insurer about the occurrence of the insured event on time is logical and fundamental obligation of the insured party. Without this notification credit insurer most probably cannot be acquainted with these facts and circumstances which affect the insured, and thus he cannot pay the claim. To notify the occurrence of the insured event as soon as possible is often necessary to ascertain whether the loss-causing event is also the insured event, covered by the insurance policy, and even more to launch proper debt collection and subsequent recovery activities expeditiously.

- Under credit insurance conditions for **commercial risk cover** the duty of the insured to submit the request for claims payment for his outstanding trade receivables against insolvent buyers usually arises with the institution of the bankruptcy or rehabilitation proceedings (i.e., occurrence basis).
- On the other hand, when the debtor is not declared to be **permanently insolvent** and **protracted default** is also covered as usual the insured has to file the request for claims payment after the lapse of the **waiting period** as defined in general or special insurance conditions for covered protracted default of the debtor, for example, 6 months. This period may commence the day after the date of the insured's previous notice on overdue debts in accordance with the insurance conditions (i.e., claims-made basis), or at the date of the last partial payment effected after such notification. The insured may, for example, also file his request for claims payment after the lapse of 180 days time period after the due date for the first and the oldest invoice unpaid by the buyer.

SUBMITTED DOCUMENTATION. In addition to the original of the insurance policy when individual credit is insured and in accordance with general insurance conditions, the insured must submit filled-up and signed **request for claims payment** form (claim form) with the statement of the occurrence of a particular insured event, summary of the circumstances and the list of unpaid invoices. Whereas paper form is still in use, information society and competitive environment is putting more emphasis on e-commerce and high-speed communication between the insured and his insurer also in claims handling procedures *via* Internet.

By the rule, it may be also requested to enclose additional documents or their (true) copies that satisfactorily evidence covered credits, the occurrence of the insured event and the loss sustained, etc., for example:

- underlying commercial contract, purchase order, invoices, shipping, customs and other documents or their (true) copies—including (an

authenticated) translation as appropriate—evidencing the dispatch, existence and validity of the trade receivables, their outstanding amounts and currencies, delivery and payment terms and conditions;
- documents evidencing the occurrence of the insured event, for example:
  - buyer's recognition of the debt;
  - petition of the debt in insolvency procedure;
  - final court order or decree of an administrator for institution of insolvency proceeding, or their acknowledgment of the debt owed or repartition of the bankrupt's estate;
  - evidence of an unsuccessfully concluded execution; and
- other documents evidencing proper performance of the obligations of the insured company, that is, dunning letters, correspondence with the debtor and notes on telephone conversations, lawsuit, (verified) transcript or statement of the accounts of the buyer in certain period of time (e.g., 2 years prior to issuance of the first invoice from the request for claims payment), documents that justify discretionary limit decisions, etc.

Credit insurer may demand case-by-case also some other documents, such as documents or their copies related to eventual ROT, bills of exchange (B/E) or promissory notes, bank guarantees, and similar undertakings issued by third parties, etc.

General insurance conditions *inter alia* also state that the insured event may occur when

- the consent of all creditors to out-of-court settlement is given,
- with the lapse of time period of, for example, 90 days from the submission of evidence that the measures against the debtor or his assets would be uselessness or unsuccessful,
- there is no prospects for repayments and institution of court procedures against the debtor, and
- when salvage sales contract was concluded in agreement with the insurer as a result of imminent occurrence of the insured event.

In case of protracted default insurance cover the evidence of the occurrence of the insured event is easier for the insured. Waiting period or protracted default, for example, 3, 6, 9, or even 12 months in riskier countries, commences the first day after the reported overdue trade receivables.

LOSS-CAUSING EVENT. Already from the Roman law it is a well-known rule: *"Causa proxima, non remota spectator."* In general, it holds true also for credit insurance that the insurer shall pay the claim if the insured event is a proximate and not a remote cause of loss. Credit insurer is liable only if the loss-causing event—which represents the insured event under the applicable insurance conditions—is a **proximate cause of loss**. Therefore, the insured event must be a direct, active, effective, and dominant cause of material loss incurred to the insured.

PRI. If credit insurance is restricted to cover commercial risks only and insurance policy does not provide cover against political risks—for example, convertibility risk—and these noncommercial risks are thus excluded from insurance coverage for the exporter, credit insurer would not be liable for losses caused by such events and would not pay claim. In disputes between the parties of the insurance contract— nevertheless, these risks should have been a proximate and direct cause of loss always—the burden of proof (*onus probandi*) that the loss incurred is the result of uncovered political risks rests with the insurer. On the other hand, when the policy covers also political risks and the insured is able to prove that such event actually prevented him to get payment and the debtor did everything necessary to effect payment— for example, he had deposited contract amount in local currency and provided all the documents—the insurer would pay claim on the basis of PRI or comprehensive insurance cover. Despite for the insured in general it makes no difference on which basis the claim is paid so far it is paid without complication, except perhaps where the insured percentage or waiting period may differ, this nevertheless might be important anyway. The example would be in case the export credit insurance against nonmarketable risks is provided by the ECA on the state account, while marketable risks are covered on its own account.

It is always possible that the payment default is a consequence of many loss-causing events when each of them may also represent the insured event, for example, debtor's bankruptcy as a result of commercial risks and more or less simultaneously occurred covered political risks. In such a case credit insurance does not entitle the insured to multiple claims payments on the basis of each and every insured event, unless various events would lead to partial losses. Losses attributable to the same credit are usually indemnified under the principle that the claim is paid on the basis of the insured event which occurred first, or the credit insurer may deduct from the claim paid all the sums covered under other insurances—if such insurances are exceptionally not prohibited by applicable credit insurance conditions. Should a political and a commercial risk occur simultaneously or in close connection with each other the loss may be also considered to have been caused by the insured event which represents political risk.

LOSS SUSTAINED. Property insurance including credit insurance is indemnity insurance. Credit insurance indemnifies the insured company with the agreed claims paid for direct material losses incurred *(damnum emergens)* due to buyer's payment default, that is, the insured percentage of the loss sustained excluding consequential losses, including but not limited to loss of production, loss of contracts and markets, lost profit *(lucrum cessans)*, etc. The loss incurred usually equals to the amount of overdue debts, that is, invoice amounts which may include packing, freight and insurance costs, excluding or including VAT and similar taxes and charges. The claim amount is decreased by counterclaims of the debtor which can be set off and other proceeds from the debtor—including any monies received from the enforcement or realizations of guarantees and other securities—preserver sales under ROT and dividends paid from the bankrupt's estate or composition. The principles governing the contracts of indemnity lead to the conclusion that credit insurance does not entitle the insured to enjoy unjust enrichment with the multiple claims payments.

DOCUMENTATION. Required documentary evidence enclosed to the insured's request for claims payment may differ from one insurer to another and even case by case. As already said, the insurer may *inter alia* also request:

- true transcript or computerized records of the accounts of the insured's business with the buyer before the first unpaid invoice issued;
- all other documents related to the insured event, for example, correspondence with the buyer, his objections, documents related to debt collection activities and their costs, protested bills of exchange, given guarantees and other securities, etc.; as well as
- other documents needed for claims handling and recovery of the claims paid.

The insured company must timely submit the request for claims payment with full set of documents evidencing the occurrence of the insured

event, the amount of covered loss incurred and costs for its prevention and minimization as well as his right for claims payment.

4.4.2 Ascertainment of Loss

Because the active function of credit insurance (see in Section 2.2.2)— that is, the indemnification for losses incurred due to insolvency of the debtor or protracted default and minimization of adverse consequences of the loss-causing event—is its basic and the most important function, emphasis on quick and efficacious claims handling is very important for the insurer and his competitiveness and crucial especially for the insured company. The insured counts on cash flow whether from his credited debtor or from the compensation from the insurer. Illiquidity may harm his business, hinders the fulfillment of his obligations, threatens his creditworthiness and reputation, and on the other hand, external bridge financing if available may be costly for him. Nevertheless, credit insurance, especially export credit insurance, and claims handling are usually not very easy and simple. Firstly, a credit insurance policy is not an unconditional instrument, and on the other hand, for example, business relationships between the contracting parties may be complicated, documents are often in foreign language, applicable laws can be unknown or untested, foreign jurisdiction can be involved, etc. Therefore, claims handling in the credit insurance business may be demanding and may sometimes inevitably last some time. To shorten these difficult stage and procedures as much as possible and to get claims paid it is important for the insured to file his request for claims payment and complete documentation in due time.

●●●───────────────────────────────────

> **Incompleteness of documentation is the most important reason for *slow* ascertainment of losses and pretentiousness in claims handling procedures.**

In ascertainment of losses **legal and claims departments** usually thoroughly check submitted requests for claims payment and required documentation enclosed by ascertaining their foundation basis and amount of the claims paid. In claims handling procedures credit insurers and their claims examiners give special attention *inter alia* to the following facts and questions:

- Has been the claim form of the policyholder or authorized beneficiary with the required complete documentation and evidence submitted in time, for example, in 6 months after the occurrence of the insured event?

- Does this request relates to covered credit and debt of the buyer with the set and valid credit insurance limit and has the loss incurred during insurance cover period and before the insurance limit expired?
- Was the credit properly reported and due insurance premium and charges paid?
- Has the credit been granted or have the goods been dispatched and services rendered or invoiced after the expiry of maximum extension period despite the prohibition of overtrading after the buyer has already been in default for this or another overdue debt?
- Does the insured have a valid and legally binding claim and is there a dispute between the parties of the underlying commercial contract regarding the existence of the debt, its validity, and/or amount?

Payment default, nonpayment and payment delays or other improper payments are judged according to their underlying contracts and applicable rules of the governing laws. If applicable rules prescribe that certain deficiencies or infringements of the debtor's payment liabilities represent his fundamental breach of contract the insurer would regard such improper payments, for example, different currency, place or mode of payment, as nonpayments and will pay the claim in accordance with applicable insurance conditions.

As already said (see Section 3.2.5 in Chapter 3), this conditional financial instrument does not provide protection against performance risk of the seller and covers only credit or payment default risk of the buyer. If there is a dispute between the contracting parties about the validity and amount of the debt owed or justified objections and counterclaims of the buyer exist, normally the insurer shall temporarily reject the request for claims payment until the settlement of the dispute is reached and the final decision about the buyer's liability is established. Because of its conditional nature credit insurance cannot extend its effects beyond *nomen bonum* protection. Therefore, for valid and unencumbered trade receivables underlying commercial contracts and provisions of governing laws retain great importance even for credit insured sellers. The first best option is usually to negotiate open issues with the counterparty, but if this attempt is not successful, the insured seller may need to (last) resort to *ad hoc* or institutional arbitration or litigation in the court. By all means it is preferable to resolve the dispute in fair manner speedily and not to litigate under jurisdiction of the buyer's country. In such case credit insurance cannot help much and the matter retains in the sphere of the insured company and his contractual relations under underlying commercial contract. Anyway, the insurer will usually pay an undisputable amount of claim and he can also pay part of the claim on account (provisional and conditional payment of claim against recourse agreement), if appropriate.

Last but not least, it is also logical that credit insurance company is never obliged, unless specifically agreed otherwise, to pay claim for the loss or part of the loss sustained that is deliberately or by negligence caused, contributed or increased by the insured himself or by any person acting on his instructions or from his sphere (e.g., consortium partners, forwarding agents, and banks). The opposite would usually be unfair, against the good faith and in contradiction with mandatory civil law provisions *(contra legem)*. Moreover, it would be also against the rule in insurance that the loss-causing event must be uncertain and independent from the will of the parties of the insurance contract.

- Is nonpayment related to the insured debt of the buyer?
- Is the loss-causing event also the insured event as defined in insurance conditions?

Let us repeat about noncommercial or political risk cover that the named insured event—for example, volcanic eruption or civil war—should actually prevent the buyer to effect payment and not only makes the fulfillment of his obligations more onerous. Because the risk and insurance is about the future and uncertain perils, the claim shall not be paid, for example, for losses due to preexisting import prohibition if it is enacted before the PRI cover commences. On the other hand, PRI normally does not cover losses to the extent that the policyholder has been able to get "normal or customary" insurance cover for these perils elsewhere, for example transport and other property insurances.

Which risks are covered under credit insurance conditions are usually interpreted restrictively *(interpretatio limitata)*. But unclear and inaccurate provisions of general and special insurance conditions are in doubt by the rule interpreted in favor of the insured and against the insurer who is a professional and can normally be blamed for their wording.

- Is the loss incurred excluded from cover by a particular exception?

  Onus of proof rests with the insurer. He has to produce the evidence from which it can be reasonably argued that the event occurred falls within the exclusion and that this directly or indirectly caused the loss and only then the insured is required to disprove it.

- Has the insured properly fulfilled all of his duties and obligations under the insurance contract and complied with insurance conditions?

  Among these fundamental obligations of the insured it is worth mentioning again for the claims handling the following duties which can in practice often lead to rejection of the insureds' requests for claims payment:

  - prompt and perfect disclosure and reporting—prior to the conclusion of the insurance contract as well as during the insurance policy period—of all material facts and circumstances that may influence the risks underwritten and risk assessment as well as possibility and efficacy of the measures and activities for loss prevention and minimization;
  - to act prudently and to comply with agreed delivery and payment terms and conditions approved by insurance policy or credit limit decisions including maximum credit terms, and not to allow their extension beyond agreed maximum extension period or changes—including waiver of creditor's rights, debt rescheduling, write-offs, etc.—without the approval of the insurer;
  - to regularly declare all of his trade receivables and outstanding debts of the debtor and other buyers subject to set insurance limits;
  - to refrain from overloading;
  - to pay insurance premium and charges due;
  - notifications on (untolerated) payment delays by the time specified in the policy and cessation of deliveries to such buyers, if not agreed otherwise with the insurer;
  - to launch debt collection activities, to protest unhonored B/E and to follow the insurer's instructions in debt collection; etc.

Credit insurers and their legal and claims departments usually check and may verify all these and also other relevant issues. After all, trade receivables are usually one of the most important assets of the company, and on the other hand, credit insurance claims may be big and heavy burden for the insurer. Moreover, moral hazard can always exist in trade credit insurance and therefore the insurers also reserve their rights to inspect books, records and documentation of the insured parties. That is why the claims handling in credit insurance can be quite demanding, especially if the insured company does not have its business operations, sales, accounting, finances, and credit risk management properly organized and documented. This inevitably also aggravates claims handling and poor credit insurance policy management is definitely not in the interest of the insured.

When, for example, the bank guarantee or surety bond is a condition for credit insurance cover, the insurer shall normally not ascertain the loss until their unsuccessful realization or until a final court judgment or arbitral award for the amount owed is obtained against the issuer.

It is very important for the insured to comply with insurance conditions and not to have the claim rejected because of failure to observe imposed conditions and duties of the insured after the contracts are concluded, the insured event occurred and insured suffered uncomfortable loss without the benefits from his insurance policy. The things can go wrong but do not need to. It is always useful to set up credit control and credit insurance procedures and documentation as well as to establish a system—computerized, as appropriate—to remind the insured on key deadlines for his duties related to credit insurance policy and claims handling.

4.4.3 Claims Payment

According to insurance conditions the insurer has to pay claim to policyholder, for example in 30 days after he receives the request and complete documentation for claims payment that evidence the occurrence of the insured event and the amount of loss incurred.

INDEMNIFICATION. The claim is paid upon fulfillment of insurance conditions and up to the amount of **overdue debts** not exceeding **insurance limit** set for the buyer as an indemnification for the loss incurred for his all and accumulated outstanding overdue debts. This compensation is reduced proportionately to the agreed percentage of cover or **self-retention** of the insured and other deductibles, if any. In the same proportion and in addition to **claims paid** the insured is usually also entitled to **compensation for costs** related to his **debt collection** and **recovery** activities. Moreover, some insurers even pay higher claims if debt collection is started early.

Occurrence of the insured event and claims paid at the latest have also an outcome that the credit insurance limit for that buyer is canceled automatically. Subsequent deliveries, if any, are therefore not covered.

Credit insurer may refuse to pay claim in full or partly if ascertainment of loss indicates that he is not obliged to accept the insured's request for claims payment. The insurer's liability is not unconditional and is dependent upon occurrence of the insured event and performance of the duties of the insured party. Especially in case of heavy and recurring violation which entitle the insurer to deviate from general principle of the contracts to preserve the contracts notwithstanding the infringements of the parties *(favor contractus)*, the insurer may terminate or revoke insurance contract.

In certain cases the insured may be able to negotiate a settlement with the insurer. In other cases, the claim not being paid can be a lesson to make changes in credit (insurance policy) management and to avoid losing a claim for the second time in future. Anyway, if the insured is convinced about his rights he can always challenge the insurer's opinion and go to court. But the litigation is most probably not very good for his future cooperation with the insurer who would not like to jeopardize his reputation and may try to avoid that.

RULE OF PROPORTIONS. Compensation for loss sustained can be reduced when the insured caused the occurrence of the insured event or contributed to increase of the loss incurred. The same is also true for his **underdeclaration** where the **rule of proportions** is usually applied in claims handling, that is, the insurer pays claim in proportion to the declared turnover and insurable turnover that should have been declared, but it was not with the alleged inspiration to save on insurance premium paid. A claims department thus checks the share of undeclared debts already paid by the date of ascertainment of loss in whole insurable turnover of the insured in the same period of time and the claims paid are proportionately reduced for the share of not declared trade receivables.

Example:
- Set insurance limit—EUR 100,000, self-retention—15 percent, declared and overdue trade receivables (bankruptcy of the buyer)—EUR 80,000, undeclared and unpaid overdue trade receivables—EUR 20,000 (for the sake of simplicity the VAT is not covered).

    The insurer pays: claim = EUR 54,000 (EUR 80,000 × 0.8 (EUR 100,000/EUR 80,000) − EUR 9,600 (15 percent) = EUR 64,000 − EUR 9,600)

On the other hand, the insurer pays claim for declared and actually granted credits only, and not for eventual excessive declarations of the insured's turnover over the actual one. In such a case suspiciousness about insurance fraud can exist with possible sanctions also for criminal offense.

In most of the life and property insurances, except for liability insurance, the *all or nothing* **rule** is applied. This rule, as sometimes also *ex gratia* **claims payment**, wins recognition in credit insurance as well. When it is questionable whether the basis for and the insurer's liability exist or not credit insurance company does not decrease the amount of claims paid.

If the final amount of the loss incurred is not yet known at the occurrence of the insured event and submission of a claim form, the insurer shall pay undisputable part and appropriate **provisional claim**. The amount of provisionally paid claim can rise by the time in line with eventual increase of undisputable loss incurred. Of course, the insured must always reimburse the insurer for overpayments and this right is usually guaranteed by special **recourse agreement** and even personal and real securities, especially if these claims are paid for questionable losses to another beneficiary (assignee) under the assignment of insurance policy rights.

Especially in such blatant case the insurer may insist upon signing of a special *assignment declaration* of the insured prior to his claims payment. Such declaration may be included in the agreement between the parties of the insurance contract on their consent to payment of claim and covered costs incurred, their amount and conditions. This agreement usually also contains special provisions with the duties of the insured to allocate and transfer to the insurer all subsequent proceeds from the recoveries of the debt proportionately to the insured percentage and waiver of the rights and future claims of the policyholder as a condition to claims payment.

Currency of Account/Payment and Exchange Rate Risks

Pecuniary obligations of the credit insurance contract parties including payment of insurance premium, claims payments and recoveries may be affected by mandatory and other provisions of monetary and civil/commercial laws as well as—in international trade, business with the nonresidents and where the place of payment is abroad—by applicable foreign exchange laws. Governing laws prescribe what legal tender is and in which currencies monetary obligations of the parties can be denominated and/or executed.

Monetary obligations are usually stipulated and fulfilled in domestic currency of at least one or even both parties of credit insurance contract being legal tender, by the rule in domestic credit insurance, or may be—in export credit insurance—in accordance with insurance conditions and mandatory laws also executed and/or expressed in convertible and freely usable foreign currencies. These currencies of the export credit insurance contracts will be usually the same as the currencies in underlying commercial transactions (invoice currency). In export credits the buyer's payment obligation is thus often denominated in foreign currency. This foreign currency can be a currency of payment, that is, free of exchange clause, or may be a currency of account only—when such protective currency clause as a *tertium comparationis* or *numéraire* is stipulated—which is used to calculate the final amount (countervalue) of the debtor's payment settled in currency of payment. For this calculation and conversion contractually agreed exchange rate can be used, or official (published) exchange rate, for example, valid in the place of payment at the date of each invoice or its maturity or at the payment day as prescribed by the contract or/and applicable monetary laws.

Monetary obligations of the parties of the credit insurance contracts shall be—in the open space of possibilities and admissibility of various currency clauses including those which use composite currency units, for example Special Drawing Rights (SDRs)—defined in insurance contracts and general insurance conditions in accordance with the rules of the governing civil or commercial and foreign exchange laws and regulations.

As a consequence of the worldwide applicable principle of monetary nominalism and as a result of economic laws and monetary policy, monetary obligations, except in spot transactions, inevitably carry additional noncommercial monetary risks (currency or exchange rate, interest rate, and inflation risks), that is, the risk of changes in internal and/or external value of currencies (depreciation/appreciation), depending on what is used as a yardstick. As long as we deal with international trade and several national currencies sales on credit terms are indispensably exposed to exchange rate risk and business operators use various economic, financial, legal, and combined instruments for hedging and protection of their transaction exposure. Credit insured companies can also be protected *mutatis mutandis*. But this is not always necessary. By definition exchange rate risk does not exist in domestic credit insurance and where the monetary obligations are denominated in domestic currency. On the other hand, credit insurance usually covers short-term commercial transactions where this risk is more or less trivial as long as there is a stable economic environment. And finally, exchange rate risk linked with export credit insurance may be under control when, for example, for the claims payment various protective currency clauses are agreed in accordance with general insurance conditions.

Credit insurance cover is usually provided in hard currencies and such currency clauses may also apply for monetary obligations of the insured party, for example, payment of insurance premium is specified in countervalue of the declared trade receivables denominated in foreign currencies.

4.5 RECOVERIES

Distinction and **difference between claims and losses** are one of the features that distinguish credit insurance from majority of other types of nonlife insurances. Sometimes in credit insurance when the claim is paid this loss of the insurer is considered as a final or effective one if there is, for example, no bankrupt's estate available to repay the debt, and then we talk about the **dead loss** on which no further recovery is possible.

IMPORTANCE OF RECOVERIES. However, things are often not so bad in credit insurance and credit insurers may expect to recover rather substantial portion of their claims paid over time, for example, around 10 percent from insolvent buyers and about 30 percent of commercial risk claims on average (usually it is higher when the claims are paid for protracted default) and sometimes even much more of political risk claims. Until the recovery is made, the claim paid is considered unrecovered while the claim paid, or part of it written off or anticipated to be irrecoverable, can be classified as a net loss in applied accounting terms when no further recovery is considered and this also influences the insurers' provisioning. Rarely in commercial risk insurance claims paid are from the very beginning or initially regarded as dead losses and it may take long time for the insurers to finally recognize the net loss. That is why their annual cash-flow figures might be misleading and this has additional effect that in addition to collected premium recoveries are very important source of revenues or secondary income for credit insurers; for some ECAs recoveries have even surpassed insurance premiums on their new business insured.

As recoveries are very important in credit insurance business, it is worthwhile to recall that the cooperation between the insurer and the insured party does not end with the claim payment but is continuing with the insurance cover for other business of the insured as well as with actions to recover claims paid which requires involvement of the insured and that is also one of the duties of the policyholder.

4.5.1 Subrogation

After the occurrence of the insured event credit insured seller usually has at least two independent claims:

i. against the buyer—the debtor and his guarantors on the basis of their underlying commercial or credit contract, and
ii. against the insurer under the credit insurance policy, while sometimes hypothetically there can be also the third claim, for example,
iii. against the person who caused the loss on the basis of his liability.

Therefore, the company has for the loss incurred alternative demand *(ius variandi)* to get compensation from both of them. But it would be against the principles of indemnity if the policyholder can accumulate his claims, except when he is not fully indemnified from one of these debtors, that is, in addition to claims paid the insured can get from his debtor a part of his debt which exceeds the claim paid for the insured's self-retention.

Claims paid by the insurance company do not release the *main debtor* from his payment liabilities under the commercial contract. The contrary would be illogical, unfair, and against public order. Credit insurance contract is stand-alone and is not accessory to underlying commercial contract as surety bonds. Anyway, with the claims paid by credit insurance company the insured creditor is indemnified and the insurer may become subrogated in his rights, privileges, remedies and actions against the debtor. Such personal **subrogation** *(subrogatio)* has a goal to ensure the possibility for the insurer (subrogee) to recover claims paid and pursue the main obligor whose payment default caused the loss incurred to the insured (subrogor) and indemnified creditor. Nevertheless, the loss sustained is finally to a large extent borne by the insurer.

Under general principles of law *ex lege (cessio legis)* and under insurance conditions upon payment of claim credit insurer may automatically *ipso iure* enter—up to the amount of the claims paid—into all and any rights of the insured creditor against the debtor, including accessory rights from given securities.

ASSIGNMENT. Alongside to already mentioned **assignment declaration** in Section 4.4.3—this one of the personal subrogation and the policyholder's consent to claims payment with the waiver of his rights is usually silent and the debtor is not informed about it without the insurer's consent—**the insured party (transferor) may also specifically transfer his rights against the debtor in writing *(cessio voluntaria)* to facilitate the insurer's (transferee) debt collection and recoveries**, including endorsement of B/E and promissory notes, assignment of rights from issued guarantees and other personal securities relating thereto. Furthermore, the insured is under an obligation to do everything necessary to enable the insurer to exercise such rights. The credit insurer may then use such assignment to demonstrate and assert his rights against the debtor or to whoever is obliged to pay the debt, for example, his legal successor or insolvency practitioner, in court or out-of-court proceedings. Of course, transferred rights are not the insurer's "own" rights but are originated in and derived from crediting seller's rights. Therefore, the debtor retains against the insurer all the objections that he had against the creditor. Multiple transfers of creditor's rights are usually also allowed thus the insurer may further assign these rights to the third party, such as debt collection agency, and may also reassign these rights back to the insured. By this way such person may then assert these rights against the debtor directly.

4.5.2 Recovery Activities
Without subrogation to insured creditor's rights and recoveries of at least part of the claims paid credit insurance premiums would definitely be higher for desired technical result of the insurer and consequently credit insurance would be more expensive for the insured parties.

In accordance with general insurance conditions even after the claims payment the policyholder has to cooperate with the insurer and must follow his instructions for activities and measures to recover the claims paid against the debtor and his legal successors.

If he does not comply with insurance conditions the insurer may request the reimbursement of the claims paid and can realize securities given for his right of recourse.

After the claims payment and signing of the assignment declaration the insured must accept all effected payments and partial payments from the debtor or guarantor including monies emanating from bankrupt's estate and sale of collateral, if any, and must remit them immediately or as soon as reasonably practicable to the insurer, in full or partly if agreed so, according to insured percentage and his self-retention. Recoveries are allocated first to the outstanding invoices with the earliest due dates. For all payments effected before the claim was paid the insured has to reduce his request for claims payment as well as the value of goods returned to him before or after the claim payment is deducted from the credit amount. **Abandonment** with its tradition in marine insurance is normally not known in credit insurance, except otherwise is explicitly agreed, and the insurer is usually not obliged to take over credited goods and pay full amount of claim *(compensatia lucri cum damno)*. Instead, for the value of goods returned the loss incurred is reduced.

The insured has to bring any appropriate salvage action against the debtor and/or his guarantor, for example, attaching and seizing the assets of the debtor in default (prelitigation recovery). If it is practical and necessary he has to sue as well as to file his petition and take part in bankruptcy and other proceedings, especially when they are solvent and successful decision can be expected sooner or later. As already mentioned (Section 4.4.1), in accordance with general insurance conditions the insured needs to register his debts in insolvency proceedings in order to prove the existence of the valid accounts receivable or debt owed to him, which has not been set off, etc. If this is requested the insured has to assist the insurer in his actions against the debtor including the appointment of the insurer as his agent or attorney with power to take legal proceedings in his name.

Costs for recovery activities—including legal fees and charges—are, as already said (see Section 3.2.4 in Chapter 3), covered as well.

Founded external costs of recovery activities are shared between the insurance contract parties proportionately to their agreed share of loss sustained (e.g., 85/15) or it is divided between them at the same ratio as between the amount of the credit insured and the claims paid. Sometimes insurers even contribute to recovery costs if the debtor pays his debt when the policyholder can demonstrate that the measure avoided the loss.

As for their shares in the loss sustained, the insurer and the insured also share recovered sums after claims payment, for example, default interest, compensation for damages, proceeds of resale, dividends from bankrupt's estate after the expenses and any other salvage. Recovered amounts go first for debt collection costs of those who borne them—either the insurer or the insured party—and the rest is allocated between them *pro rata* as to the insured and uninsured percentage; but it may be agreed that the insurer takes precedence over the insured.

Thus for the insured company indemnification for loss incurred may be even increased by his share in recovered amounts added to the claims payment.

4.6 INSTEAD OF A CONCLUSION

INSURANCE POLICY MANAGEMENT. As explained in Section 4.3.1 and elsewhere, credit insurance policy management requires active involvement of the insured party, his well-organized day-to-day activities and intense cooperation with the insurer during the policy period. Credit risk is inherent to contemporary commerce and does not need to come as an outrageous surprise even if the company is not risk averse. Of course, some other alternative methods of protection might sometimes better suit the company's needs. But if it is credit insured, it is better to bear fruit from a bought insurance policy and to be able to make a valid claim, if needed.

As we have seen, credit insurance requires frequent personal interactions between both parties of the insurance contract and is labor intensive. On the other hand, it is also conditional financial instrument despite it can be very useful and is considered as efficacious protection tool against payment default risk. But bear in mind, however, that credit insurance may deeply affect the business of the company and that credit insurance policy is also subject to various insurance conditions that must be complied with to get the claims paid for the losses incurred; and this is, nevertheless, the most important function of credit insurance.

Credit insurance policy management is usually a long-term ongoing process with changes, development and gradual adaptation to changes in risks underwritten, trade pattern of the insured and experience gained in this cooperation between the parties of the insurance contract, claims experience and changing needs and approach of the policyholder. It is therefore always useful to analyze all these and to suggest appropriate changes, if needed.

RENEWING THE POLICY. The best time for all these is usually before the end of insurance policy period—normally, short-term credit insurance turnover policies have a standard duration of 12 months from the inception date—at its renewing. Firstly, the insured has to gather information regarding values of his past trade volume and business insured as well his envisaged or forecasted future figures by his customers and their countries in line with his trade strategy and business plans. Secondly, these figures should be complemented with the amounts of claims paid and recovered and their comparison with the costs of credit insurance over the period divided to insurance premiums, fees and charges for insurance limits, debt collection, etc. Finally, this experience and the company's own track record are useful to analyze efficiency of credit risk management and for renewal negotiations with the existing insurer or another one, if the policyholder decides not to continue the cooperation with the same credit insurance provider, or even to decide to switch completely or partly to other methods of protection and alternative instruments (substitutes).

Equally important is to check set insurance limits (as already said, if the financial situation of the buyer or his country deteriorates substantially, the insurer may withdraw the cover for future business, or may impose additional conditions and restrictions), maximum credit terms and conditions as well as the insurance premium levels. It is important that insurance conditions match underlying commercial contracts and changed circumstances and trade pattern of the insured including his new products and services with different credit terms, new customers, and new markets. Here it is worth mentioning again that the insurer will oppose adverse selection of risks and will insist to cover whole turnover or spread of risks but will be normally willing to switch to some variations, for example, excess of loss policies or even selective forms of insurance cover, to tailor his services to the insured's own sophisticated credit risk management, exposure and appetite for risk.

To have included in cover traditional customers only and also not risky countries with not too narrow risk portfolio will definitely contribute to lower premium rates. Of course, insurance premium rates may rise if the policyholder's claims ratio is unfavorable, his credit risk management proved not to be good and if the credit or country risks worsen. As we have already seen, claims ratios are very important ingredients in the formula for insurance premium calculations. Such increase of premium rates may even lead to abandonment of credit insurance and consequential higher exposure to losses or withdrawal from some markets. In *ultima linea*, if claims ratio deteriorates and if claims paid, claims under consideration and potential claims increase the insurer may be unwilling to renew insurance policy. On the other hand, despite a good claims record may be remunerative in regard to insurance premium rates it is usually not worth to orient the trade to first class buyers only and not to expand trade with less worthy but still solid customers, or to never file the claim at all.

Changes in credit insurance conditions can have dramatic effect on sales and risk management. Therefore, they need to be thoroughly analyzed and taken into account by all departments and staff involved. Here we do not mean only changed insurance limits and risks covered, but also, for example, the transfer from a loss occurring to risk attaching insurance policy and *vice versa* where the insurance gaps that can be created for some accounts receivable or to pay for double insurance should be avoided. About these and other matters, such as high insurance limits and claims, an advice of experienced **credit insurance broker** and advisers can bring the benefit to the insured companies and can help to get more from credit insurance providers.

CHAPTER 5

Advantages of Credit Insurance

Credit insurance is developed as a flexible and high-quality integral financial instrument of protection against payment default risk of the buyers, and for many business operators it is suitable and superior to other virtually equivalent or imperfect substitutes that serve similar financial needs or protection, but might sometimes also be complementary, for example, real and other personal securities as well as some alternative capital market instruments, that is credit default swaps (CDS) and asset-backed commercial papers (ABCP). Credit insurance fosters trade and enables the companies selling goods and/or rendering services:

- to create additional purchasing power with the safe crediting of the buyers and expands their sales to the existing and new customers in domestic market and abroad;
- to be competitive on the markets with the sales on credit terms and payments on open account;
- to facilitate external financing of their business operations by the banks and other financial institutions;
- to successfully manage and mitigate their credit risks in line with their business strategy and policies; and
- to use credit insurance policy as an efficacious and rather simple and not expensive device for transferring the credit and country risks to specialized and financially strong credit insurance company and thus creates required economic and financial security.

Credit insurance, for example:

- boosts sales and creates potential for **growth** to benefit from challenges and opportunities on demanding markets;
- ensures **competitiveness** of the sellers with favorable payment terms offered, that is, deferred clean payment without required additional and costly securities;
- enhances **financing** (supplier credits, bank loans, etc.) and paves the way for better payment terms and conditions, acquisition of working capital, hiring loans, and other external financing under more favorable terms and conditions;

Credit Insurance. DOI: http://dx.doi.org/10.1016/B978-0-12-411458-6.00005-8

- with the transfer of risks to credit insurer the company may achieve required economic security, improved **creditworthiness**, and higher credit rating;
- noticeably improves companies' cash flow and **credit risk management** that can seriously threaten their liquidity, profitability, value of their assets (accounts receivable), and even their mere existence;
  - Quality and up-to-date **credit information** on buyers, their branches and markets as well as regulations in force, and permanent **risk monitoring** enable the insured to adopt appropriate business policy and to alter their sales and crediting policy. On the other hand, this information obtained from the credit insurer may be of better quality and less expensive.
  - Credit information is not just the recommendation but are "upgraded and fortified" with the set credit **insurance limits** backed by the insurer. These limits prevent excessive accumulation of outstanding debts and help the company to adopt and run its sales policy as well as to decide on appropriate crediting and payment terms and conditions.
  - Credit insurance decreases likelihood of payment default and insured credits are better repaid in practice than unsecured debts.
  - **Debt collection** with the assistance of credit insurer is facilitated, proved to be more efficient, successful, and less costly.
    The same is also true for **recoveries** of the claims paid and by the sums recovered of the claims paid for the losses incurred may consequently be even increased for the insured company.
- Credit insurance policy provides economic security for the insured company and its trade receivables with the **indemnification for the loss incurred**. Guaranteed claims payment enables the insured to plan his business and cash flow needed for undisturbed business operations—with credit insurance policy in hand "unpredictable cash flow can be transformed to certainty"—and can help to win confidence of his customers, banks, and other business partners.
- Credit insurance policy is a rather simple safeguard financial instrument that does not overburden the insured with too much of additional **administration** as long as he is well organized and has a good credit risk management applied.
- Furthermore, credit insurance is usually **price competitive**—typically short-term credit insurance premium rates are in the range of

0.1–0.5 percent and more—and also brings some other important advantages over other instruments of protection against the risk of nonpayment. These instruments may be more or less perfect substitutes for credit insurance but may be sometimes employed also as an additional or parallel security.

For riskier markets, credits with longer tenor and for problematic buyers certain collateral—for example, ROT or bank guarantee—may be requested as a condition for valid credit insurance cover. Such additional securities may also have an impact on set insurance limits, insurance premium rates, and other insurance conditions.

- Credit insurance does not guarantee safe trade and does not provide quality financial services only, but in addition to financial guarantee of a credit insurance company for indemnification of the loss sustained it also provides sometimes even more important auxiliary services. Such outsourcing is cost-effective and insured companies can remain focused on their main activities, that is, product development, acquisition of new customers, and so on. These related extra services, for example, credit risk assessment and monitoring, debt collection, and so on, may be included in serviced credit insurance and are a good basis for long-term business relationship between the partners and the parties of the insurance contract.

Invoice Discounting and Factoring

Credit insurance policy is a financial instrument being issued by specialized financial institutions, but it is insurance and not a financing instrument even though it may facilitate financing. Thus, unlike the assignments of accounts receivable (*cessio voluntario*)—for example, discounting B/E and promissory notes, forfaiting, invoice discounting, and factoring services—credit insurance directly does not serve as a trade finance instrument.

Invoice discounting is a banking business whereby the bank on the basis of individual and large enough invoices raised on buyers with the acceptable risks advances an agreed proportion of the invoice value; normally higher if the trade receivables are insured. The buyer's payments to the bank as a nominee, rather than to the seller, are retained by the bank in the amount financed and the balance less the costs and fees are remitted to the seller. The arrangements—mainly used for short-term working capital—differ and the percentage of the debt financed as well as the banks' rights of recourse may vary.

On the other hand, **factoring**—mainly provided by specialized factoring companies and now increasingly internationalized—as a hybrid financial product with integral financial services, and especially its broadest form, that is, nonrecourse (conventional/old line) factoring, can be a complement to credit insurance as well as more or less perfect substitute or tantamount alternative to credit insurance, but in practice we can find also **credit insured factoring**. In comparison with credit insurance, at least in theory, factoring can be—notwithstanding the development of these services and their supply, prices, flexibility, presence on the markets, and so on —even superior financial instrument. Factoring combines various (optional) financial and auxiliary services for the sellers (clients), for example, administration of the sales ledger, credit information, risk monitoring, debt collection, legal consultancy, and so on, and can provide protection for their trade receivables against credit and currency risks (factoring without recourse to the seller/exporter), with added additional and its main function (with the exception of maturity factoring)—asset-based financing of sellers' or exporters' working capital needs (prepayment of part of the purchase price of the debts).

Credit insurance and value added of insurance services provide the policyholder required economic security and savings. On the other hand, credit insurance is a lucrative business and economic security does not come for free. Specialization of credit insurers and fierce competition on credit insurance markets as well as substitutes put insurance premium rates at relatively low and competitive level. Nevertheless, irrespective of the credit insurance premium rate applied, the cost for credit insurance cover is very rarely prohibitive and can be easily built in the price for goods sold on short-term credit. At least in long-term period, collected credit insurance premiums are normally appropriate compensation for these services and therefore this instrument with its powerful elements of risk management is usually competitive.

●●●———————————————————————————

Credit insurance policy is usually worth the money spent for it.

———————————————————————————————

Insurance v. Self-Insurance

Smart farmers in "years of fat cows" make reserves for bad times. Similarly is also true for the companies; part of their revenues or profits from successful operations in the past they usually retain as a contingency fund for future expected or unexpected damages or at least prepare themselves for the "known unknowns."

With the transfer of manufacturing and/or credit risk to financial institution—credit insurance company, because of harsh competition on the market, the law of large numbers, and better spread of risks as well as due to specialization of credit insurers, credit insurance is certainly superior to self-protection and self-insurance. Nevertheless, self-insurance can prove to be useful protection device against noninsurable risks, in case of underinsurance and for protection of the insured's self-retention in the loss sustained.

There is not much space for efficacious self-insurance because of its inferiority, very competitive credit insurance market, and the nature of credit risks. Moreover, self-insurance always threatens the self-insured with possible bigger losses that may seriously harm his balance sheets. The best chances for self-insurance are with the actuarially predictable risks with high frequency of small losses, but on the other hand, self-insurance requires sufficient time and sources for risk management.

This is similar for big companies and multinationals if they decide to formalize their cost advantages of self-insurance in established (single—parent or profit—center) **captive insurance company** to reduce transactions costs and save on premiums and because of other financial and tax reasons (premium payments to captives can be deducted). Captive insurance company may then also cede its risk portfolio to reinsurance market. But credit insurance is rather difficult insurance class for captive insurance companies since specialization and special know-how is required, credit information and country-risk assessments are needed as well as professional debt collection and recovery activities might be demanding.

Because by self-insurance, the self-insured company creates economic security with the levelling of the risks by itself self-insurance in fact is not insurance. The losses are always borne by self-insured and the risks are not transferred to third party. The self-insurance does not mean the transfer of risks, but it is a mechanism to protect the self-insured against their consequences just to better or easier cope with them. Therefore, the protection of the self-insured is not external and is more or less an apparent protection. One can also talk about self-insurance as "a (much) less or the least primitive kind of noninsurance."

Although some often see self-insurance as the biggest competition to credit insurance—and this competition can even increase with better accessibility of good credit information—this is not true gold. In fact, main competition to credit insurance is still ignorance, that is, neglected and underestimated credit risks in business practice. Ignorance presumes where knowledge is timid.

- Self-insured or noninsured company saves credit insurance premium but has to rely on its own internal resources for credit risk management, it has to pay for credit information and debt collection, its provisioning needs to be established on the basis of different figures and built-up general provisions are normally not tax deductible. On the other hand, credit **insurance premium is allowable against taxable profits** and eliminates the need for excess contingency funds. Thus, credit insurance policy can be used to replace provisions and reserves against doubtful accounts receivable to increase profits.
- Another important merit and advantage of credit insurance policy usually lies in the fact that it is **oriented on credit risk portfolio and whole turnover**, or at least substantial part of it, of the insured company. Videlicet, credit insurance rarely covers selected accounts and individual business transactions that require each time a separate or different instruments for protection, special agreement between the parties of the underlying commercial contract, as well as an involvement of the third parties, negotiations on terms and conditions of given securities, etc.

Bank Instruments

With the merit to cover the entire or a substantial part of short-term trade and to manage credit risk portfolio of the insured company, credit insurance can offer much lower prices than substitutive bank instruments that are mainly issued to cover individual transactions, for example, bankers' acceptances, various payment and service **bank guarantees**, and commercial or stand-by **letters of credit** (L/C). As an invention and creation of international business and banking practice, these outstanding financial instruments are hardly regulated but are subject to applicable rules of autonomous international law and trade usages published by International Chamber of Commerce (ICC).

These well-established and frequently-used methods of efficacious protection against payment and counterparty risks are issued on global and local levels to back up a wide range of debtors' financial and nonfinancial liabilities stemming from various kinds of underlying relationships but are normally issued individually to cover single business transaction. Backed by reliability and financial strength of their issuers and their obligations, which are usually unconditional and legally independent from the existence, validity, and enforceability of the main debtors' obligations from the underlying commercial or financial contracts these rather simple financial instruments with the issuer's original, primary, and independent liability without doubt have many advantages. An L/C, for example, is a nonaccessory undertaking of the bank given to the crediting seller and issued on the instruction of the applicant (debtor/buyer) to pay at sight or at a determinable future date a stated amount of money upon complying demand and presentation of requested shipping and other title or nontitle documents.

The quality of these bank instruments and their wide use in contemporary business transactions with the lack of trust and inherent commercial and noncommercial risks are understandable, but they also have some disadvantages. So as to not only praise these instruments, let us proceed with some of their deficiencies.

Briefly, bank instruments are normally issued—except, for example, global guarantees—to cover individual transactions. Therefore, bank instruments usually cannot be a comprehensive or complete solution for the creditors' problems and can resolve their problems with nonpayments or payment defaults of the main obligors only partially.

To get bank instruments can be time consuming—therefore, it is clear that they are not suitable for last-minute orders—and considerably costly for the companies. Moreover, they also require involvement and activities of their counterparties, for example, customers. On the other hand, if issued, they increase transaction costs and burden credit limits of the applicants and may reduce their overall credit availability considerably. Moreover, requested collateral for right of recourse of the guarantor or issuer may immobilize sources of the company needed for other business, and all these may have negative impact on its borrowings and competitiveness. Furthermore, bank instruments are not always the best solution for both parties—the creditor and the debtor, and are usually less convenient for small transactions and for less sophisticated companies. Although, in general, irrevocable L/C—frequently used especially in international trade with unknown buyers from difficult markets—efficiently removes possibility of the buyers' payment default and also protects the buyer because the bank will not pay unless the correct full set of requested documents evidencing performance of the seller will be presented, this does not exclude all the risks. For instance, precredit risks and political risks that may prevent payment from the importer's bank if the L/C is not issued or confirmed by the first-class bank domiciled in the exporter's country.

On the other hand, particularly if the company is less experienced with this documentary instruments there may be also some "hidden costs," inconvenient paper work, and risks associated with the requested (strict) compliance of timely presented documents with the credit or guarantee conditions. Documentary conditions may cause delay in supplying goods and increase costs for warehousing, sometimes the exporter is not able to present requested documents issued by third parties (PCR insurance can provide cover for such manufacturing risks), or the documents are missing or inconsistent with the requirements. In practice, a lot of first presentations are rejected, requiring their revision and representation, and if the seller misses scheduled dates for shipment the L/C must be amended, etc. Moreover, credit or bank guarantee documents might be forged, they can be lost and cannot be submitted on time, or can be "clean" despite the goods are not as such. Furthermore, underlying commercial contracts may be terminated or canceled already before the L/C is issued, etc.

Therefore, there can be many problems with the bank instruments and even frauds and disputes among the parties may arise. There are problems in business practice with false, incorrect, and incomplete instructions, failures of the parties, extensions of expiry of these instruments, and disagreements about related costs.

Bank instruments such as L/C and bank guarantees can be seen as substitutes and competition to credit insurance with their strengths and weaknesses over credit insurance and as more or less appropriate solution for particular company and its business. On the other hand, bank guarantee and L/C can also be a complement to credit insurance policy and are sometimes required as a precondition to insurance coverage. Bank guarantees are, for example, often employed in medium-term export credit insurance business, but must be thoroughly stipulated, issued by the acceptable bank on simple or first demand with its unconditional liability independent from underlying credit transaction, and sometimes also transferable to lending bank or credit insurer.

- Unlike the above bank instruments, credit insurance policy covers named insured events and it is a conditional financial instrument subject to many insurance conditions that must be complied with to get the claims paid after the expiry of the waiting period. Moreover, covered loss incurred is normally not reimbursed in full but up to the insured percentage (self-retention is borne by the insured himself).
- On the other hand, credit insurance may be a very good response for the trade problems and trends on many markets where companies face harsh competition and where we can witness a switch from secured trade on credit terms and wide use of bank instruments to expanding and prevailing **open account deliveries**.
- Like undisclosed factoring, credit insurance is a **discreet instrument** that does not endanger mutual trust as well as business and collegial relationships with the customers and business partners. In

general, credit insurance improves a buyer's access to supplier credit facilities and supports trade on open account that presumes trust to the debtor and does not require involvement and cooperation of the insured's customer. A buyer is usually not even aware that a tiny insurance premium is included in the contract price, and neither the insurer wants the buyers to think that they do not need to pay because the claim will be paid to the insured seller anyway.

* Buyers are usually reluctant to be disturbed with activities that concern the sellers, especially to provide them the instruments for protection that are costly and may exhaust their credit limits.
* Trade credit can "serve as a warranty" and credit insurance is "**customer-friendly instrument**" that enables the buyer to inspect delivered goods before the payments, whereas sales on open account terms do not require from the buyer to furnish the creditor with the securities.
* The buyer purchasing goods on credit terms and open account shall not try to include the costs for nonrequested securities and lay them on seller, with the request to reduce the price.
* And last but not least, credit insurance is, as a matter of fact, practically the only disposable instrument that provides security also for the debtor or borrower. Unlike L/C and bank guarantees, credit insurance is not an unconditional instrument with the primary and independent liability of their issuer, that is, specialized financial institution, which can be honored regardless of improper performance or failure to fulfill the seller's or lender's obligations.

In general, among basic payment terms and conditions the following instruments used in trade finance are advantageous to the seller/ exporter (in descending order):

* cash with order (CWO)
* advance payment
* promissory note/B/E
* surety bond
* irrevocable (independent/confirmed) bank guarantee/stand-by letter of credit (stand-by L/C)
* documents against irrevocable confirmed payment order (D/ICPO)
* confirmed irrevocable letter of credit (CIL/C)

- irrevocable letter of credit (IL/C)
- revocable letter of credit (RL/C)
- documents against payment (D/P)/CAD
- documents against acceptance (D/A)
- cheque
- **sales on deferred payment (credit) terms on open account.**

At the top, *vice versa*, one can find the least favorable payment terms and conditions for the buyer. Sales on credit terms on open account are the most favorable for the buyer. Market and negotiating positions are nowadays generally in favor of buyers. On a so-called buyers' market, the trade is thus financed by the sellers using either their own or external sources. Therefore, to be successful they are pushed to offer their goods to privileged buyers on deferred and clean payment terms. Buyers' unbalanced and open position may be well rectified with credit insurance providing efficacious protection against payment defaults.

Credit insured sales on credit and open account terms enable competitive trade, that is, deferred payment terms without additional securities. That will be blessed by the buyer while the crediting seller is efficaciously insured against his payment default due to commercial and noncommercial risks inherent to contemporary trade.

BIBLIOGRAPHY

A Report on the Provision of ECGD Reinsurance for Exports Sold on Short Terms of Payment, ECGD, London, July 2000.

Bakker, M.H.R., Klapper, L., Udel, G.F., 2004. Financing Small and Medium-Size Enterprises with Factoring: Global Growth and Its Potential in Eastern Europe, first ed. World Bank, Warsaw, Poland.

Ball, J., Knight, M. (Eds.), 1989. The Guide to Export Finance. Euromoney Publications, London.

Bastin, J., 1998. Bonajuto Paris SANGUINETTI premier théoricien de la protection contre l'insolvabilité (Sa biographie/Son œuvre)—Deuxième edition, Fondation Scientifique Jean Bastin A.S.B.L., Spy.

Bertrams, R.I.V.F., 1988. Bank Guarantees in International Trade, second revised ed./second reprint. ICC Publishing S.A./Kluwer Law International, Paris/New York/The Hague/London/Boston.

Biais, B., Gollier, C., 1977. Trade credit and credit rationing. Rev. Financ. Stud. 10 (4), 903–937.

Bickelhaupt, D.L., 1974. General Insurance, ninth ed. Richard D. Irwin, Homewood.

Birds, J., 1988. Modern Insurance Law, second ed. Sweet & Maxwell, London.

Brau, E.H., Puckahtikom, C., August 1985. Export Credit Cover Policies and Payments Difficulties, IMF Occasional Paper No. 37, Washington, DC.

Briggs, D., Edwards, B., 1988. Credit Insurance—How to Reduce the Risk of Trade Credit. Woodhead-Faulkner, New York/London/Toronto/Sydney/Tokyo.

Carter, R.L., Lucas, L.D., Ralph, N., 1999. Reinsurance, fourth ed. Reactions Publishing Group/ Guy Carpenter & Company, London.

Chauffour, J.-P., Malouche, M. (Eds.), 2011. Trade Finance during the Great Trade Collapse. World Bank, Washington, DC. Available from: <http://siteresources.worldbank.org/INTRANETTRADE/ Resources/TradeFinanceEntire.pdf>.

Communication of the commission amending the period of application of communication of the commission to the member states pursuant to article 93(1) of the EC treaty applying articles 92 and 93 of the treaty to short-term export-credit insurance—2010/C 329/06 (OJ C 329, 7.12.2010).

Communication of the commission to member states amending the communication pursuant to article 93(1) of the EC treaty applying articles 92 and 93 of the treaty to short-term export-credit insurance (OJ C 325, 22.12.2005).

Communication of the commission to the member states pursuant to article 93 (1) of the EC treaty applying articles 92 and 93 of the treaty to short-term export-credit insurance—97/C 281/03 (OJ C 281, 17. 9.1997).

Conference: Insuring Export Credit and Political Risks (British Exporters Association), Inn on the Park Hotel, London, March 30–31, 1992.

Credit Insurance for European SMEs: A Guide to Assessing the Need to Manage Liquidity Risk, European Commission—DG for Enterprises, Brussels, 2003.

D'Arcy, S.P, Doherty, N.A, April 1990. Adverse selection, private information and lowballing in insurance markets. J. Bus. 63 (2), 145–164.

Dowding, T., 2000. Developments in Credit and Political Risk Insurance, ICIA Credit Insurance Review, London.

Eiteman, D.K., Stonehill, A.I., Moffet, M.H., 2010. Multinational Business Finance, twelfth ed. Prentice Hall, Boston, MA.

Export Credit Insurance and Guarantee Schemes—A Practical Guide for Developing and Transition Economies, ITC, Geneva, 1998.

Export Credit Insurance, Munich Re Group, Munich, 2000.

Funatsu, H., June 17, 1984. Theory of Export Credit Insurance (Dissertation Presented to the Graduate Faculty of Dedman College of Southern Methodist University).

Global Credit Management, The NCM Group, Amsterdam, 2000.

Goode, R., 1995. Commercial Law, second ed. Penguin Books, London.

Haniotis, T., Schich, S., 1995, September. Should Governments Subsidize Exports Through Export Credit Insurance Agencies? UNCTAD Discussion Papers, No. 103, Geneva.

Hawkins, D., 1999. Business of Factoring: A Guide to Factoring and Invoice Discounting. McGraw-Hill, London.

Jiménez, G., 1997. Export–Import Basics, ICC Publication No. 543(E), Paris.

Jus, M., 1999. The Nature and Insurability of the Exchange Rate Risk, IB revija, vol. XXIII, No. 4/1999, UMAR, Ljubljana, 45–52.

Jus, M., 2004. Kreditno zavarovanje, Založba Sanje, Ljubljana.

Kumar, M., 2000. Export credit insurance: an analysis. Asia Insurance Post. Available from: <http://www.einsuranceprofessional.com/artcredit.html>.

La prévention de la défaillance de paiement, Actes du 2e Congres Sanguinetti 1998, Larcier 2000, Bruxelles.

McKenna, E.J., 1983. Surety Underwriting Manual, 6th ed. Rough Notes, Indianapolis, IN.

Merkin, R.M., McGee, A., 1988. Insurance Contract Law. Kluwer Publishing, Kingston upon Thames.

Retention of Title, second ed. ICC Publication No. 501, Paris.

Rowe, M., 1987. Guarantees, Standby Letters of Credit and Other Securities. Euromoney Publications, London.

Rowe, M., 1997. Letters of Credit, second ed. Euromoney Publications, London.

Sallinger, F.R., 1991. Factoring Law and Practice. Sweet & Maxwell, London.

Schmidt, C., 2006. Credit Insurance and Surety: Solidifying Commitments, Sigma, No. 6/2006, Swiss Re, Zürich.

Schmitthoff, C.M., 1990. Export Trade, ninth ed. Sweet & Maxwell, London.

Smith, J.K., 1987. Trade credit and informational asymmetry. J. Finance 42 (4), 863–872.

Stephens, M., 1999. The Changing Role of Export Credit Agencies, IMF, Washington, DC.

The BExA Guide to Export Credit Insurance, British Exporters Association, London. Available from: <http://www.bexa.co.uk/exportinfo.html>.

The Export Credit Financing Systems in OECD Member and Non-Member Countries, OECD, Paris.

The Economic Rationale for the Public Provision of Export Credit Insurance by ECGD (A Report for the Export Credits Guarantee Department), NERA, London, April 2000.

Trade Credit Insurance: Globalisation and e-Business are the Key Opportunities, Sigma, No. 7/2000, NCM, Amsterdam, 2000.

Van der Veer, K.J.M., October 2010. The Private Credit Insurance Effect on Trade, DNB Working Paper, No. 264/2010, Netherlands Central Bank, Amsterdam. Available from: <http://siteresources.worldbank.org/INTRANETTRADE/Resources/Internal-Training/287823-1256848879189/6526508-1283456658475/VanderVeer.pdf>.

White, R.J., 1987. Guide to ICC Uniform Rules for Contract Bonds and Model Forms (ICC Publication No. 536 (E)), Paris.

Wilsher, R., 1995. Export Finance—Risks, Structures and Documentation. Macmillan, Chippenham.

WEBSITES

http://www.alasece.com

http://www.aon.co.uk/tradecredit

http://www.apfpasa.ch

http://www.atradius.com

http://www.berneunion.org.uk

http://www.bexa.co.uk

http://www.coface.com

http://www.ecb.int

http://www.ecgd.gov.uk

http://www.edc.ca

http://www.einsuranceprofessional.com

http://www.eulerhermes.com

http://www.factors-chain.com

http://www.hbor.hr

http://www.i-law.com

http://www.iccwbo.org

http://www.iciece.com

http://www.icisa.org

http://www.ifgroup.com

http://www.journalofcreditrisk.com

http://www.mapfre.com

http://www.oecd.org

http://www.sid-pkz.si

http://siteresources.worldbank.org

http://www.swarb.co.uk/lisc/Insur19801984.php

http://www.vanuatu.usp.ac.fj/courses/LA313_Commercial_Law/Cases

http://www2.zav-triglav.si

CPSIA information can be obtained at www.ICGtesting.com
Printed in the USA
BVOW03s0513110913

330869BV00015B/132/P